Almost a Territory

Almost a Territory

America's Attempt
to Annex the Dominican Republic

William Javier Nelson

DELAWARE

Newark: University of Delaware Press
London and Toronto: Associated University Presses

© 1990 by Associated University Presses, Inc.

Associated University Presses
440 Forsgate Drive
Cranbury, NJ 08512

Associated University Presses
25 Sicilian Avenue
London WC1A 2QH, England

Associated University Presses
P.O. Box 488, Port Credit
Mississauga, Ontario
Canada L5G 4M2

The paper used in this publication meets the requirements of the American National Standard for Permanence of Paper for Printed Library Materials Z39.48-1984.

Library of Congress Cataloging-in-Publication Data

Nelson, William Javier.
  Almost a territory : America's attempt to annex the Dominican Republic / William Javier Nelson.
    p.   cm.
  Includes bibliographical references.
  ISBN 0-87413-380-7 (alk. paper)
  1. Dominican Republic—Annexation to the United States.   2. United States—Foreign relations—Dominican Republic.   3. Dominican Republic—Foreign relations—United States.   4. Dominican Republic—Politics and government—1844–1930.   5. United States—Foreign relations—1865–1898.   6. United States—Territorial expansion.
  I. Title.
  E183.8.D65N45   1990
  327.7307293—dc20
                                                              89-40204
                                                                  CIP

PRINTED IN THE UNITED STATES OF AMERICA

*This book is dedicated
to my parents,
Amelia Beatrice Dinkins Nelson
and Colonel William James Nelson,
for their unfailing selflessness and support.*

Contents

Author's Note

If the reader discerns in this work a preponderance of U.S. government sources and records, as well as evident emphasis on North American participants, he or she should not argue with those impressions. The story of the unsuccessful 1868–71 struggle for the annexation of the Dominican Republic to the United States is not one of a great Dominican uprising against "Yankee imperialists." Although many Dominicans, some of them prominent citizens, fought against annexation, the proponents of the annexation themselves, the most influential of whom were North Americans, set into motion those factors that caused its ultimate defeat. In terms of the ability to resist a U.S. takeover, the Dominican people were no more capable than the people of the Philippines, Alaska, or Puerto Rico—all of which became United States possessions. Moreover, Dominican President Buenaventura Báez was successful in creating and maintaining a government stance officially in favor of annexation. The fight over annexation in many ways came down to a test of political strength between two heroes of the Union cause in the U.S. Civil War.

It is difficult for any analyst of Dominican history to escape the sense of Dominican helplessness as compared to the strength of the United States. The events in this narrative will not greatly alter that conclusion.

Acknowledgments

Several people have greatly helped me at several stages of my research. I would especially like to thank my very good friends Francisco Rafael Baret Martínez and Diómedes Alcides Pérez Peña for their help. I was also aided by some timely advice from Professors Joel Smith and Peter H. Wood of Duke University, both of whom I have known as my mentors for over fifteen years. Dr. Pedro Ramón Vásquez y Vásquez graciously submitted to two personal interviews and allowed me the use of the facilities of the Archivo General de la Nación de la República Dominicana, of which he is director general.

I gratefully acknowledge the help of Dr. Peter Fraser of Goldsmith College, London, whose interest in Dominican affairs matches mine. My close friend Eddy Herman Davis helped give me a framework by which to compare life in the Dominican Republic and the United States. I am indebted to Dr. Luis E. Martínez Rodríguez for use of some rare Dominican volumes. I will not forget Dr. Luis Ernesto Pérez Cuevas's willingness to interrupt his busy schedule and travel with me to various parts of the Dominican Republic as I sought out information.

Although it would not be possible to list here all the libraries that provided me assistance and information, the following gave invaluable data: the Yale University Library; the Moorland Spingarn Center of Howard University through its archivist, Esme Bhan; the Boston Public Library rare books sections; the University of Florida Library; the Duke University archives section; and the University of North Carolina Library at Chapel Hill. Of course, this work would not have been possible were it not for the facilities of the U.S. Library of Congress, particularly its public documents department, archives department, and photographic records section. The same can be said for the U.S. National Archives, especially the microform department and the manuscript department.

Some of the most important assistance I received came from Mrs. Caroline Peterson of the interlibrary loan department of Saint Augustine's College, Raleigh, North Carolina. I am also indebted to the National Endowment for the Humanities, which provided a summer grant under the direction of Dr. Doris E. McGinty of Howard University.

Above all, I would like to thank my wife, Angela, for her love and friendship, without which I could not have even started this project.

Almost a Territory

1

Introduction

El que mucho abarca, poco aprieta.

(He who tries to do it all does just a little.)
                                        —Dominican proverb

In Puerto Plata, Dominican Republic, a beachfront luxury hotel (one of many in this tourist-oriented city) carries out its functions in best mid-1980s style. It offers not rooms but suites; a hospitality director plans a plethora of activities; it even has a grocery store.

Since the Dominican Republic lies well within the path of resort areas frequented by North Americans (like Bahamas, Jamaica, and the lesser Antilles), one might suppose that the majority of the guests at this particular hotel would be wealthy natives of the United States. Indeed, some are—in fact, a large percentage are Canadian. What would surprise the casual observer unfamiliar with the area, however, is the fact that a great many of these vacationers, with their confident air and prosperous look, are Puerto Rican.[1]

Having similar language (Spanish), customs, and even musical traditions, Dominicans and Puerto Ricans nevertheless diverge in significant ways. That masses of Puerto Rican tourists vacation in nearby Dominican Republic points to a salient difference: per capita income and standard of living.[2] Puerto Rico's per capita income is almost three times that of the Dominican Republic.[3] An important factor in Puerto Rican development has been its status as a U.S. possession. Long considered one of the most backward and slum-ridden islands in the Caribbean,[4] the Spanish possession of Puerto Rico was acquired by the United States as a consequence of its victory over the Spanish in the Spanish-Cuban-American War.

The U.S. occupation had far-reaching effects. One was to firmly tie Puerto Rico, economically and politically, to the United States.[5] With the well-publicized initiatives of Luis Muñoz Marín, the first Puerto Rican politican to seriously court industry, Puerto Rico embarked upon a path of development unlike most Latin countries by moving away from subsistence farming and toward a more complex division of labor.[6] This unique status of Puerto Rico has not been problem-free. The U.S. economic presence has been suffocating, although in present-day Latin America this state of affairs is not the exclusive domain of Puerto Rico.[7] Puerto Ricans have been subject to conscription in the U.S. armed forces.[8] At present, in spite of its well-known economic miracle, Puerto Rico has depended increasingly on U.S. federal support, rather than local enterprise.[9] Puerto Ricans understandably feel politically inferior since they are denied a voice in U.S. presidential elections and reside in an "unincorporated territory" that has no independent powers granted to it by the U.S. Constitution.[10] Puerto Ricans' cultural uniqueness, compared to other citizens of the United States, has sharpened their sense of embattlement and helplessness, in spite (or perhaps because) of their increasing association with the United States.[11]

On the other hand, the Dominican Republic is an independent country, not a U.S. possession. However, had it not been for Charles Sumner, Carl Schurz, and others, the Dominican Republic—a verdant expanse of some of the most beautiful land in the Caribbean—would have been Puerto Rico's sister, a possession of the United States. This book is about the extraordinary sequence of events leading to the request of the sovereign nation of the Dominican Republic, in the years immediately after the second of its two struggles for independence, to be absorbed by the western hemisphere's rising imperialist power: the United States. Inasmuch as the United States' other possessions in the Caribbean (Puerto Rico and the Virgin Islands, for example) were colonies themselves at the time of their acquisition by the North Americans—and therefore had no real voice in the matter—the spectacle of an independent nation like the Dominican Republic attempting to annex itself to another nation points to the need to investigate both societies. What kind of leadership in the Dominican Republic of the last century would willingly offer a country for sale? What kind of populace would let that happen? What kind of nation would desire to extend its political umbrella to a country with a different language and culture? What kind of people would seek to profit from a nation's reversion into a colony?

The answers to these questions involve national imperatives, as well as the existence at that time of some colorful adventurers. The Dominican Republic had the distinction of sharing a single island with Haiti, a country with a vastly different culture, racial makeup, and history. At the time of its first independence, the Dominican Republic was extremely vulnerable, not only to other nations generally, but also to Haiti, from which it had gained its first independence. Its predominantly conservative leaders desired security by affixing their country to some powerful sponsoring nation. The Dominican Republic thus had the distinction of being led by men who fought for its independence from Haiti in order to surrender it to a powerful country like Britain, France, Spain, or the United States.

The United States was a young nation that, having settled its differences over slavery, now looked to join the other Western, advanced nations as a full-fledged power. It was also wary of European encroachment in the western hemisphere. Even before the Civil War, presidents like Franklin Pierce had expressed expansionist sentiments; moreover, the practice of filibustering was rampant. Ulysses S. Grant, the U.S. president who came closest to annexing the Dominican Republic, favored an expansionist foreign policy and had a secretary of state who was diplomatically capable of implementing the negotiations necessary for any annexation.

In addition, the fight for annexation had two formidable protagonists, both of whom were North Americans: "General" William L. Cazneau and "Colonel" Joseph W. Fabens. These men managed to manipulate both the government of Dominican President Báez and the political apparatus of the United States, including President Grant.

A study of the background, characteristics, and history of this interesting country can give the reader an appreciation of the drama that almost caused the United States to add to its territory nearly 21 percent of the total land area of the West Indies.

NOTES

1. On several visits to Dominican Republic in the 1980s I found quite a number of Canadians and South Americans, as well as Puerto Ricans.

2. Howard J. Wiarda and Michael J. Kryzanek, *The Dominican Republic: A Caribbean Crucible* (Boulder, Colo.: Westview Press, 1982), 132.

3. Ibid.

4. Preston E. James, *Introduction to Latin America* (Indianapolis, Ind.: Odyssey Press, 1964), 290–94.

5. Julian H. Steward et al., "National Patterns during the American Period, 1898–1948," in *The People of Puerto Rico*, ed. Julian H. Steward (Urbana: University of Illinois Press, 1969), 62–63. Also see Ramona Carr, *Puerto Rico: A Colonial Experiment* (New York: New York University Press, 1984), 201–11.

6. D. A. G. Waddell, *The West Indies and the Guianas* (Englewood Cliffs, N.J.: Prentice-Hall, 1967), 112–14ff. Also Steward et al., "National Patterns," 63.

7. Steward et al., "National Patterns," 63. See also Carr, *Puerto Rico*, 201–11. For a picture of U.S. economic domination of a nominally independent country, see Jaime Suchlicki, *Cuba from Columbus to Castro* (New York: Charles Scribners Sons, 1974), 83–88.

8. Steward et al., "National Patterns," 63.

9. Richard J. Bloomfield, Introduction to *Puerto Rico: The Search for a National Policy,* ed. Richard J. Bloomfield (Boulder, Colo.: Westview Press, 1985), 2.

10. Ibid., 1–2.

11. Arturo Morales Carrión, "The Need for a New Encounter," in *Puerto Rico,* ed. Bloomfield, 9–24.

2

Quisqueya

THE LAND

The Dominican Republic, with a land area of 46,759 square kilometers—compared to Puerto Rico's 8,787 square kilometers—must have seemed a big prize to the North Americans who, at various times in the nineteenth century, contemplated its annexation. Comprising the eastern two-thirds of the island of Hispaniola (the second largest island in the Caribbean), the Dominican Republic is bordered by the French-speaking Republic of Haiti. Seventy-seven kilometers northwest of Hispaniola is the island of Cuba, the largest in the Caribbean; one hundred kilometers eastward, across the Mona Passage, lies Puerto Rico.

Containing the most arable land in Hispaniola,[1] the Dominican Republic is 286 kilometers wide, from Cabo Beata in the south to Cabo Isabella in the north, and 390 kilometers long, from Cabo Engaño in the east to the Haitian frontier in the west. Although the Dominican Republic was not internationally known for fine beaches until the 1970s, it does have some spectacular shoreline. In addition to the well-known resort beaches of Puerto Plata, the country has expanses of shoreline called *costa alta* in which the land literally rises from the sea, forming gigantic green hills. The Dominican Republic, which is part of a submerged mountain chain, like the other island countries of the Greater Antilles,[2] is dominated by several ranges, all of which run northwest to southeast. From largest to smallest, they are the Cordillera Central, in the middle of the country; the Cordillera Septentrional, which fronts the Atlantic Ocean on the north coast; the Cordillera Oriental, which lies below the Bay of Samaná; and the small ranges of Sierra de Neiba and Sierra de Baoruco, which are located in the arid southwest section. The country's small rivers are formed from water drained from these various chains.

The peninsula of Samaná lies in the northeastern portion, providing a harbor and a bay—visible features that have deeply influenced

A Dominican luxury resort.

Dominican countryside. *(Photograph by author.)*

Dominican sugarcane fields.

Dominican history. In addition to the great eastern plain, the Llano Oriental—which runs from Haina to Cabo Engaño along the southern coast—the main areas of cultivation in the Dominican Republic are those fertile valleys encountered between the various *cordilleras*. The largest and most fertile valley, which has also been the scene of many important events in the country's history, is the Cibao, which includes the Vega Real. The Cibao lies in the north, between the Cordillera Central and the Cordillera Septentrional. Although there has been a movement toward diversification of agricultural production, the chief Dominican crop, for a major portion of the nation's history, has been sugarcane.[3]

Because of the diverse topographical configurations of the country and their climatic variations, the Dominican countryside is a mixture of high peaks, deserts, humid lowlands, lush valleys, and low plains. The country, while usually free of the extreme climatic conditions common to other tropical locations, is nevertheless in the path of the "hurricane channel." In 1930 the worst hurricane in the history of the Caribbean struck the city of Santo Domingo, which resulted in a tightening of newly installed dictator Rafael Trujillo's grip on the Dominican people.[4]

THE PEOPLE

The population of the Dominican Republic is predominantly mulatto. In the 1980s, 73 percent of the population was listed as mulatto, 16 percent white, 11 percent Negro, and the rest composed of other minorities.[5] These figures, however, are highly unreliable in terms of the racial nomenclatures of the United States or South Africa. For example, many of the Dominican "whites" would probably be classified as "coloured" in South Africa. In the United States, possibly 60 to 70 percent of the population of the Dominican Republic would be classified as "black" if it were not for the fact that "hispanics" in the United States are allowed African ancestry. Although color and class are strongly related in the Dominican Republic, with lighter skin associated with higher status, there is little castelike diversify,[7] which have resulted in more people living in urban than rural areas for the first time. The two largest cities, chief beneficiaries of this demographic shift, are Santo Domingo, with 1.3 million

The Dominican Republic, long tied to the cultivation of sugar cane as a major source of income, has in recent years made efforts to diversify,[7] which have resulted in more people living in urban than rural areas for the first time. The two largest cities, chief beneficiaries of this demographic shift, are Santo Domingo, with 1.3 million inhabitants, and Santiago, the chief city of the Cibao, with a population of 400,000.[8]

DISCOVERY AND EARLY HISTORY TO INDEPENDENCE

Christopher Columbus's 1492 "discovery" of America signaled the real start of Dominican history as well. The Discoverer and his followers were involved in a number of other "firsts," all of which deeply influenced the future of Hispaniola. The first Indian massacre of whites occurred in Hispaniola, having taken place on the north coast of the island as a response to the brutality of the Spaniards who were left behind when the *Santa Maria* was unable to return to Spain from the first voyage.[9] The first system of Indian slavery *(repartimientos* and *encomiendas),* a reflection of Spanish unwillingness to perform manual labor, was established in Hispaniola.[10] As a remedy, African slavery eventually was brought to the island, one of the first New World localities where this occurred.[11]

Columbus's talents as a navigator and describer of flora and fauna[12] far exceeded his skills as an administrator. Returning to Hispaniola on his second voyage in 1493, Columbus arrived with a fleet of ships that brought over fifteen hundred colonists equipped with all the skills and equipment necessary for building permanent settlements.[13] This voyage eventually led to the establishment in 1496 of the city of Santo Domingo, on the south side of the island. Although Columbus did succeed in "pacifying" the Indians, his cruelty and violence toward them (motivated by a desire for enough gold to justify royal interest[14]) together with inability to convince his Spanish subordinates that manual labor was required of them, resulted in such chaotic conditions that he was removed from the island in irons.[15]

The real development of Hispaniola came with the arrival, in 1502, of Nicolás de Ovando as governor. Carrying with him still more settlers and provisions, Ovando was able to establish an orderly administration and a continuation of the ongoing extinction of the Indians, who were by this time rapidly and irreversibly losing ground to the Spanish.[16] New towns were founded and gold was mined in increasing (though still disappointing) amounts. Under a system that included *encomiendas*—or grants of Indians to Spanish settlers—and *repartimientos*—"recruitment" of Indians for public and private work for fixed wages—the freedom-loving though passive Indians were reduced in population from an estimated three to five million at the time of the arrival of the Spanish to some sixty thousand as early as 1507 and to four thousand by 1533.[17] Within the ranks of the Spanish colonists there were sensitive persons who agonized over the plight of the Indians (and who suggested, therefore, the importation of Africans as slaves[18]), but the combination of new diseases, Spanish brutality, and the continuing refusal of the Spaniards to perform manual labor assured the Indians' doom.

Under Ovando, Hispaniola became a profitable colony. More important, under his administration and that of his successor, Diego Columbus (son of the admiral), Hispaniola became the seat of Spanish government in the New World, the first port of call for all ships from Spain, and the springboard for expeditions of exploration and conquest of Cuba, Mexico, and South America.[19] The very success of the colony as a springboard, however, spelled its demise as a viable settlement since more and more Spaniards left for these richer lands. Thus the decline of the Hispaniola's prestige and power began relatively early in its existence, in the sixteenth century, as Cuba and especially Mexico (which was subdued by Hernán Cortés by 1524)[20] became more powerful.[21] The decline was worsened by Spain's commercial battles with other European powers, which resulted in an era of piracy, privateering, and contraband trade. Spanish ships and possessions were vulnerable to raids and piracy, partly because of the official Spanish policy of resisting free trade with partners other than Spain. Moreover, the colony at Hispaniola was especially at risk since it possessed all the liabilities of any Spanish colony but by the midsixteenth century was reduced to the status of an island outpost with few resources on hand to offer any sort of defense.[22] In 1586 the Englishman Francis Drake plundered the city of Santo Domingo, looting and pillaging at will.[23]

The Spanish could not maintain the strong garrison needed to secure the island from foreign encroachment. This eventually led to the establishment of French settlements on the western end of the island, which the local Spanish militia (called *cincuentenas*) could not effectively control or halt.[24] After 1640, French refugees settled in Port Margot, their first base in Hispaniola, and in 1697 France eventually forced Spain to cede the western end of Hispaniola in the Treaty of Ryswick.[25] The unique division of the island that eventually resulted in two cultures, languages, traditions, and racial configurations grew out of this French presence on the western third of Spain's first New World colony. Henceforth the Spanish portion to the east (the antecedent of the Dominican Republic) would be called Santo Domingo while the French western part—the forebearer of Haiti— would be known as Saint-Domingue. This division has affected Dominican affairs to this day.

Within a few years the French built the West Indies' richest colony[26] by relying on the brutal exploitation of African slave labor. By the time the French colony destroyed itself at the end of the eighteenth century, it contained thirty-thousand whites, forty-thousand half-castes, and over half a million blacks—sixty percent of all slaves in the French Americas.[27]

In the meantime, the Spanish part of the island continued a relatively sleepy existence. Although Spain had laid the foundations for a political order with an *audiencia* (first set up in 1511 to avoid the necessity of appealing directly to the crown) and the institutions of the *ayuntamiento* (municipal corporation) and the *cabildo* (town council)[28], the stark isolation and bankruptcy of Spanish Santo Domingo made these political organizations more style than substance. The seventeenth century had been an extremely impoverished time for Santo Domingo. Racked by vulnerability to raids, exploitation by Spanish economic policies—which included abandonment of coastal villages to limit the smuggling of imports that Spain could not supply[29]—and a failure of institutions such as the religious orders and the educational system to provide the basis for independent thought, Spanish Santo Domingo became a society dominated by rural *caudillos*, or chiefs, who ruled over a servile population. Ironically, the general impoverishment of the population, together with the relative inefficiency of the slave system,[30] helped level racial differences to a degree unknown in French Saint-Domingue. During the years of raids, Santo Domingo could ill afford to reject the help of any person of color in its defense.[31] The result was the making of a society possessing the infrastructure of Spain, with its stratified, vertical hierarchy, but in reality responsive chiefly to the whims of major rural landowners. As Sumner Welles wrote:

> The 19,000 square miles of the Spanish colony were parceled out in great plantations. . . . The head of each plantation was virtually a dictator, responsible only unto himself. The difficulty in the means of communication alone prevented the colonial government from maintaining any effective supervision over the colonists. . . . In the cities and towns, life was not far different.[32]

At the time of the slave revolt in Saint-Domingue in 1791, Santo Domingo had enjoyed a revival of sorts. Its population had increased to around 125,000, compared to 6,000 in 1737.[33] It had developed an economic relationship with Saint-Domingue, selling meat and hides to the French in exchange for manufactured goods and some agricultural products.[34] The country also contained within its population greater manageable percentages of amicable racial and social groups than existed in Saint-Domingue.[35] Nevertheless, the Spanish colony even then exhibited tendencies that frequently worked against development in later times: a lack of cohesion and consensus but a willingness to follow the strongest local *caudillo*.[36] Then and in the years to come, Santo Domingo would be vulnerable to internal and external enemies.

According to Dominican historians Valentina Peguero and Danilo de los Santos, the revolt that took place on the western end of Hispaniola, which resulted in the elimination of the white population, was a five-part war. It was:

1. social, a struggle between masters and slaves;
2. racial, a confrontation among whites, blacks, and mulattoes;
3. civil, a rivalry between mulattoes led by André Rigaud and blacks led mostly by Toussaint L'Ouverture;
4. international, a fight involving ex-slaves, France, Britain, and Spain; and
5. of national liberation, a crusade that led to the establishment of the first Latin republic in the New World in 1804.[37]

Spain reacted to this situation of implicit danger to the people of Santo Domingo by ceding the Spanish portion of Hispaniola to France with the Treaty of Basel in 1795.[38] This created a power vacuum for Toussaint L'Ouverture, who was nominally representing

France but who had, by this time, amassed a considerable following among newly liberated slaves.[39] In 1801 Toussaint invaded Santo Domingo. The verdict is mixed as to the conduct of the leader and his troops, although it is generally said that later Haitian invasions resulted in the commission of many atrocities.[40] Whether Toussaint was humane or not, the Spanish exodus that had started after the Treaty of Basel began to accelerate, depriving the ex-Spanish colony of Creoles whose wealth and resources could have helped in years to come. Although Toussaint was tricked and deposed on 7 June 1802 by French Captain General Emmanuel LeClerc, who was then taking orders from Napoleon Bonaparte,[41] his successors would use his invasion and occupation of Santo Domingo as a basis for their efforts to gain control over the entire island.[42] LeClerc, although successful with Toussaint, was defeated by nature as he and most of his men succumbed to yellow fever. Soon most of the French were forced to leave Saint-Domingue.[43]

Toussaint's successor, Jean Jacques Dessalines, proclaimed the independence of Saint-Domingue on New Year's Day, 1804, as he and a group of followers declared their hatred of whites, renounced France, and gave their new country the ancient name of Haiti.[44] In time Haiti, also the world's first black republic and the second independent nation in the New World, would be forced into a chronic impoverishment.[45]

As the remainder of LeClerc's contingent left Saint-Domingue, French General Louis Ferrand disobeyed orders to leave the island and brought his troops into Spanish-speaking Santo Domingo, where he established a government.[46] Ferrand stayed until 1808, providing a modicum of order, stimulating economic activity (which included repealing Toussaint's edict abolishing slavery), and repelling another invasion from Haiti in 1805. This invasion was mounted by Dessalines and carried out under the command of both himself and his eventual successor to the mantle of Haitian leadership, Henri Christophe.[47] Ferrand was French, however, and news from Europe that Spain was being called upon to resist Napoleon's armies resulted in a general feeling among the Spanish-speaking colonists that the general had outlived his usefulness. A revolution headed by a Creole named Juan Sánchez Ramírez ended with Ferrand's suicide and the placing of Santo Domingo under a thirteen-year rule by Spain that was so inept that Dominican historians have referred to it as *España Boba* (Silly Spain).[48]

During the thirty years between the echoes of the first drums sounded by the rebelling slaves of Saint-Domingue and the November 1821 proclamation of the "Independence of Spanish Haiti" by

Santo Domingo Lieutenant Governor José Núñez de Cáceres, the illiteracy, isolation, and rural character of the Spanish colonists had scarcely improved. Their desire to join other Spanish-speaking colonists in the general wave of revolutions against Spain that was taking place throughout the western hemisphere could not be supported by force, as was happening elsewhere in Latin America. However, the real enemy of the people of Santo Domingo was not Spain but Haiti. Revolutionary hero Simón Bolívar, who had been aided by one of Dessalines's two successors, Alexandre Pétion, and who in fact had even visited the island in 1815, was unable to do more than look on as Haitian forces invaded Santo Domingo shortly after Núñez de Cáceres's declaration.[49]

Haitian ruler Jean-Pierre Boyer, Pétion's successor in the mulatto Haitian south and in power since Pétion's death in 1818, had been able to combine into one office the authority once exercised by Henri Christophe in the north and Pétion in the south. After Christophe's death in 1820, Boyer further surpassed his predecessors when his victorious troops subdued Santo Domingo and allowed him to assume command of the entire island in 1822.[50] In fact, the brevity of the "independence of Spanish Haiti" has been one of the reasons why Dominican historians have not marked this period as the true start of their country.

Depending upon the slant of the writer (which would include level of racism), descriptions of the ensuing twenty-two-year Haitian occupation of Santo Domingo range from those emphasizing Boyer's abolition of slavery to those portraying the Haitians as barbarians.[51] Most, however, agreed that the population in the Spanish part of the island was made darker as a result of both Haitian miscegenation and the exodus of more Spanish colonists.[52] Most also agreed that the chronic ills of educational deficiency, lack of consensus, and the sense of isolation from the rest of the world, Latin or otherwise, were not significantly alleviated. Most agreed too that there was little economic development during that time, if for no other reason than the fact that the same phenomenon was happening in Haiti.

Juan Pablo Duarte, a young Creole who had spent his early years in Europe, started a movement on 16 July 1838 among some of the younger and more energetic men of Santo Domingo. This movement was initially known as *La Trinitaria*.[53] Originally composed of nine men, the group worked to gain supporters by allowing new members to know only the identities of those persons responsible for their own inductions. Despite setbacks, Duarte and his followers eventually made slow progress. In 1841, natives of Santo Domingo residing in Venezuela gave financial help; in 1842, earthquakes in both the eastern and western portions of the island provided still more confusion that aided the cause of the revolutionaries, and in 1843, in part because of Duarte's aid, anti-Boyer Haitians were able to remove the long-time Haitian president from office.[54]

In spite of the fact that Boyer's successor, Charles Hérard, was also inclined to hold on to Santo Domingo, Duarte and his men now had a greater opportunity for bolder action. In addition, there were now a number of Haitian liberals who supported the Santo Domingo revolutionaries.[55] Rather than using secret passwords and symbolism in theatrical productions, the revolutionaries now openly advocated change. On 24 March 1843 Duarte, with Francisco del Rosario Sánchez, Ramón Mella, and others (including Haitian liberals) demanded constitutional and administrative reform.[56] Hérard was able to temporarily crush this revolutionary thrust, but on 27 February 1844 one hundred revolutionaries (without Duarte, who was recovering from illness in Curaçao) seized the fortress of the Puerta del Conde in the City of Santo Domingo and forced the Haitian commander, General Desgrotte, to capitulate.[57] Shortly afterward the other major cities surrendered, and on 14 March 1844 Duarte arrived on the island to claim the victory. The Dominican Republic was born.

As the Haitian troops retreated westward, partly because of the capitulations and partly because of another revolution taking place in Haiti itself (that of General Jean-Louis Pierrot against Hérard), they committed the same types of atrocities as had Haitian forces under Dessalines and Christophe.

U.S. historians have made much over America's weakness at the end of its struggle for independence. Perhaps a case can be made for such reasoning when the powerful country of today is compared to revolutionary America. But the new Dominican Republic had significantly more internal deficiencies and a much greater external threat than the United States ever encountered. The new nation still had all its earlier problems: dispersion of people over wide areas; lack of consensus and cohesion; general lack of national loyalty; and educational, political, and religious bankruptcy.[58]

In addition, Haiti was still a real menace. Haiti was in such mortal terror of reenslavement that in 1825 it had put itself in debt to France for sixty years simply to obtain French recognition of Haiti's right to exist as an independent nation. The Haitians looked eastward with the anticipation that any foreign presence on the island would result in slavery. Consequently Haiti could be expected to mount an invasion, with all its attendant horrors, at any time.[59] Whatever economic progress that had been built over the latter part of the eighteenth century and revived briefly by Ferrand had disappeared after decades of strife and misrule.[60] Perhaps most important, the infant country had a serious schism in leadership, pitting liberals like Duarte and his followers, who wanted outright independence, against conservatives such as Pedro Santana and Buenaventura Báez, who felt that only with the protection of a powerful foreign nation could the Dominicans be shielded from the Haitian threat.

Since the Dominican Republic won its independence with the aid of both France and Haitian liberals,[61] the rationale of the protectionists would not seem farfetched, especially when one takes into account the fact that even the most idealistic liberal was aware that complete independence, without foreign protection, would mean an extremely difficult struggle against Haiti. Many protectionists, moreover, had still another motivation for their stance, one that would appeal to selfish but crudely practical men: the prize of being a ruler of a strong power's colony as opposed to being the embattled president of a weak country. Given the basic nature of the protectionists (compared to idealistic liberals), it should come as no surprise that the liberals, instrumental in inciting rebellion against the foreign government of Haiti, nevertheless had little chance for success against the Dominican protectionists.

Within a few short months the protectionists stripped from power and exiled most of the important liberals, including the man known as the father of his country, Juan Pablo Duarte.[62]

NOTES

1. Wiarda and Kryzanek, *The Dominican Republic*, 5.

2. Nathan Havistock and John P. Hoover, *The Dominican Republic* (New York: Sterling Publishing Co., 1979), 7–8.

3. Wiarda and Kryzanek, *The Dominican Republic*, 72–73.

4. Robert D. Crassweller, *Trujillo: The Life and Times of a Caribbean Dictator* (New York: Macmillan Co., 1966), 90–95.

5. Jan Knippers Black, *The Dominican Republic: Politics and Development in an Unsovereign State* (Boston: Allen and Unwin, 1986), 55.

6. Marvin Harris, *Patterns of Race in the Americas* (New York: Walker, 1964); also William Javier Nelson, *Racial Definition Handbook* (Minneapolis, Minn.: Burgess Publishing Co., 1982), 32–34. See also idem, "Notes on Dominican Race Relations" (paper presented at the annual meeting of the Southeast Conference on Latin American Studies, Clemson, S.C., 4 April 1986).

7. Wiarda and Kryzanek, *The Dominican Republic*, chap. 6.

8. Black, *The Dominican Republic*, 4, 61.

9. See Antonio del Monte y Tejada, *Historia de Santo Domingo*, 3d. ed., 6 vols. (Santo Domingo: Biblioteca Dominicana, 1952), 1:195–97, for a description of Columbus's discovery of the massacre and how he dealt with it. Also see Otto Schoenrich, *Santo Domingo, a Country with a Future* (New York: Macmillan Co., 1918), 6; Rayford Logan, *Haiti and the Dominican Republic* (New York: Oxford

University Press, 1968), 27; and Selden Rodman, *Quisqueya* (Seattle: University of Washington Press, 1964), 7.

10. Helen Miller Bailey and Abraham Nasatir, *Latin America: The Development of Its Civilization* (Englewood Cliffs, N.J.: Prentice-Hall, 1973), 85–89; see also Logan, *Haiti and the Dominican Republic,* 27–28.

11. Bailey and Nasatir, *Latin America,* 91.

12. Joaquín Balaguer, *Colón: Precursor Literario* (Mexico City: Fuentes Impresores, 1974).

13. Valentina Peguero and Danilo de los Santos, *Visión General de la Historia Dominicana* (Santo Domingo: Editora Taller, 1981), 42.

14. Rodman, *Quisqueya,* chap. 1; also Black, *The Dominican Republic,* 14.

15. Bailey and Nasatir, *Latin America,* 82. This work contains a readable and informative account of Spanish New World settlement.

16. Schoenrich, *Santo Domingo,* 20; Franklin J. Franco Pichardo, *Los Negros, los Mulatos y la Nación Dominicana* (Santo Domingo: Editora Nacional, 1970), 7.

17. del Monte y Tejada, *Historia,* 1:274–75. See Estrella Betances de Pujadas, *Origen y Proyecciones del Protectoralismo Dominicano* (Santo Domingo: Editora Alfa y Omega, 1979), 26, who gives a drastically lower estimate of the initial Indian population at the time of the Discovery as one hundred thousand; however, to go to four thousand from one hundred thousand is in effect as bad as four thousand from five million. Also see Schoenrich, *Santo Domingo,* 20; Franco Pichardo, *Los Negros,* 7.

18. Rodman, *Quisqueya,* 17; Bailey and Nasatir, *Latin America,* 89–91.

19. Bailey and Nasatir, *Latin America,* 91.

20. Ibid., 97–102; Rodman, *Quisqueya,* 11. See Miguel León Portilla, "The Grief of the Conquered: 'Broken Spears Lie in the Roads,' " in *Latin America: A Historical Reader,* ed. Lewis Hanke (Boston: Little Brown, 1974), 55–65, for an Indian version of the conquest.

21. Bailey and Nasatir, *Latin America,* 91–93.

22. Peguero and de los Santos, *Visión General,* 67, 73; Logan, *Haiti and the Dominican Republic,* 30.

23. Emilio Rodríguez Demorizi, *Relaciones Historicas de Santo Domingo,* 4 vols. (Santo Domingo: Editora Montalvo, 1945), 2:7–108.

24. Peguero and de los Santos, *Visión General,* 111; see also Manuel A. Peña Batlle, *La Isla de le Tortuga* (Santo Domingo: Ediciones de Cultura Hispánica, 1971), 349.

25. Jacques Nicolás Leger, *Haiti: Her History and Her Detractors* (Westport, Conn.: Negro Universities Press, 1907), 32: J. A. Osorio Lizarazo, *La Isla Iluminada* (Santo Domingo: Editora del Caribe, 1953), 58–59. Osorio Lizarazo's pro-Trujillo slant does not, in this case, greatly alter his perceptions of Dominican history before independence. See also Pan American General Secretary, Organization of American States, 21 vols. (Washington, D.C.: Department of Public Information, Pan American Union, 1964), 8 *(The Dominican Republic):* 14.

26. Schoenrich, *Santo Domingo,* 28.

27. Franco Pichardo, *Los Negros,* 72. See also Médéric-Louis-Élie Moreau de Saint-Méry, *Description Topographique, Physique, Civile, Politique et Historique de la Partie Française de L'Isle de Saint-Domingue,* 3 vols. (Paris: Société de L'Histoire des Colonies Françaises, 1958), 1:46.

28. Pan American General Secretary, OAS, *The Dominican Republic,* 13–14.

29. Crassweller, *Trujillo,* 16; Rodman, *Quisqueya,* 21.

30. Peguero and de los Santos, *Visión General,* 114–15.

31. Samuel Hazard, *Santo Domingo, Past and Present* (London: Sampson Low, Marston, Low and Searle, 1873), 90–91.

32. Sumner Welles, *Naboth's Vineyard: The Dominican Republic 1844–1924*, 2 vols. (New York: Payson and Clarke, 1928), 1:1–2, 4. See also Médéric-Louis-Élie Moreau de Saint-Méry, *A Topographical and Political Description of the Spanish Part of Santo Domingo*, trans. William Cobbett, 2 vols (Philadelphia: Author, printer, and bookseller, 1796), for a French appraisal of some of Santo Domingo's shortcomings.

33. Rosario Sevilla Soler, *Santo Domingo: Tierra de Frontera 1750–1800* (Seville: Escuela de Estudios Hispano-Americanos, 1980), 28; also Frank Moya Pons, *Historia Colonial de Santo Domingo* (Santiago: Universidad Católica Madre y Maestra, 1974), 307. See also Carlos Federico Pérez y Pérez, *Historia Diplomática de Santo Domingo 1492–1861* (Santo Domingo: Universidad Nacional Pedro Henríquez Ureña, 1973), 80; Betances de Pujadas, *Origen y Proyecciones*, 27, 35–37.

34. Sevilla Soler, *Santo Domingo*, 151; Peguero and de los Santos, *Visión General*, 114.

35. Gustave D'Alaux, *L'Empereur Soulouque et son Empire* (Paris: Michel Lévy Frères, 1856), 260–61. According to D'Alaux, there were twenty-five thousand "pure" whites, fifteen thousand Africans, and seventy-three thousand coloreds at the time of the Saint-Domingue revolution.

36. Crassweller, *Trujillo*, 16–17; Welles, *Naboth's Vineyard*, 1:2–3; also Jacqueline Boin and José Serulle Ramía, *El Proceso de Desarrollo del Capitalismo en la República Demonicana* (Santo Domingo: Ediciones Gramil, 1980), 162. For a valuable glimpse of Dominican *caudillismo*, see H. Hoetink, *The Dominican People, 1850–1900: Notes for a Historical Sociology* (Baltimore: Johns Hopkins University Press, 1982), 123–25ff; and Miguel Angel Monclús, *El Caudillismo en la República Dominicana*, 3d ed. (Santo Domingo: Editora del Caribe, 1962).

37. Peguero and de los Santos, *Visión General*, 128–29.

38. Emilio Rodríguez Demorizi, *Cesión de Santo Domingo a Francia* Archivo General de la Nación (Santo Domingo: Impresora Dominicana, 1958).

39. C. L. R. James, *The Black Jacobins: Toussaint L'Ouverture and the San Domingo Revolution* (New York: Dial Press, 1938), contains a Marxist-oriented and quite graphically drawn description of the life and times of Toussaint.

40. Rodman, *Quisqueya*, 38–39, 42; see also Welles, *Naboth's Vineyard*, 1:22–24; Logan, *Haiti and the Dominican Republic*, 32.

41. Robert D. Heinl and Nancy Gordon Heinl, *Written in Blood: The Story of the Haitian People* (Boston: Houghton Mifflin, 1978), 108.

42. Logan, *Haiti and the Dominican Republic*, 32.

43. Heinl and Heinl, *Written in Blood*, 110–13; John Edwin Fagg, *Cuba, Haiti and the Dominican Republic* (Englewood Cliffs, N.J.: Prentice-Hall, 1965), 145.

44. Fagg, *Cuba, Haiti and the Dominican Republic*, 123; Heinl and Heinl, *Written in Blood*, 124–25.

45. Heinl and Heinl, *Written in Blood*, 172–73ff; Robert K. Lacerte, "Xenophobia and Economic Decline: The Haitian Case, 1820–1843," *Americas* 37 (April 1981): 499–500.

46. Welles, *Naboth's Vineyard*, 1:28–31; Rodman, *Quisqueya*, 43–44.

47. Rodman, *Quisqueya*, 42. See also Fagg, *Cuba, Haiti and the Dominican Republic*, 145, and Welles, *Naboth's Vineyard*, 1:28–40.

48. Peguero and de los Santos, *Visión General*, 145–48.

49. Welles, *Naboth's Vineyard*, 1:50; Betances de Pujadas, *Origen y Proyecciones*, 65. See also Emilio Rodríquez Demorizi, *Santo Domingo y la Gran Colombia:*

Bolívar y Núñez de Cáceres, Academia Dominicana de la Historia, vol. 33 (Santo Domingo: Editora del Caribe, 1971), 20.

50. Hazard, *Santo Domingo,* 159–71. Also Heinl and Heinl, *Written in Blood,* 159–62ff.

51. Rodman, *Quisqueya,* 46–50; Welles, *Naboth's Vineyard,* 1:51–56. See also Peguero and de los Santos, *Visión General,* 164; Black, *The Dominican Republic,* 18.

52. Stanley Walker, *Journey toward the Sunlight* (New York: Caribbean Library, 1947), 38, a Trujillist writer, also admitted that the Dominican people were made darker by Haitian rule. Moreover, Boyer deliberately undertook to darken the complexion of his Spanish-speaking colony by sending Jonathan Granville to New York for the purpose of attracting U.S. black freedmen to Santo Domingo. Although many of them died or returned to the United States, a number remained and today their descendants are found mostly in Samaná. See Hoetink, *The Dominican People,* 20–21, and also his earlier article, "Materiales para el Estudio de la República Dominicana en la Segunda Mitad del Siglo XIX," *Caribbean Studies* 7 (October 1967): 3–34, for a discussion of Granville's mission, as well as an analysis of Haitian input into the Dominican population.

53. There are many good treatments of Duarte, the most selfless of Dominican liberals. See Welles, *Naboth's Vineyard,* 1:56–73; Rodman, *Quisqueya,* 50–58; Carlos Federico Pérez y Pérez, *El Pensamiento y la Acción en la Vida de Juan Pablo Duarte* (Santo Domingo: Universidad Nacional Pedro Henríquez Ureña y Organización de Estados de Américas, 1979).

54. Welles, *Naboth's Vineyard,* 1:58; Peguero and de los Santos, *Visión General,* 170. For a look at some of the interesting Haitian reasons for Boyer's removal, see Heinl and Heinl, *Written in Blood,* 174–79, and Betances de Pujadas, *Origen y Proyecciones,* 67.

55. Welles, *Naboth's Vineyard* 1:58.

56. Ibid.

57. See Charles Callan Tansill, *The United States and Santo Domingo, 1798–1873* (Baltimore: Johns Hopkins University Press, 1938), 124n, for a glimpse of French aid on behalf of the Dominican revolutionaries, as well as for a look at the conflict between those Frenchmen who wanted a French presence in the Dominican Republic and those who feared that a truncated Haiti would be unable to pay the indemnity owed France.

58. Fagg, *Cuba, Haiti and the Dominican Republic.* See also Juan Bosch, *The Unfinished Experiment: Democracy in the Dominican Republic* (New York: Frederick A. Praeger, 1964), 135–37, for a modern Dominican impression of the church's legacy. See also Hoetink, *The Dominican People,* 153–55.

59. William Javier Nelson, "The Haitian Political Situation and Its Effect on the Dominican Republic," *Americas* 45 (1988): 227–35.

60. Fagg, *Cuba, Haiti and the Dominican Republic,* 145–47.

61. Pérez y Pérez, *El Pensamiento,* 151–75. See also Welles, *Naboth's Vineyard,* 1:58–59, and Tansill, *The United States and Santo Domingo,* 124n.

62. Pérez y Pérez, *El Pensamiento,* 151–75; Welles, *Naboth's Vineyard,* 1:66–73; Rodman, *Quisqueya,* 53–54.

1810, Báez was the grandson of the Spanish author Antonio Sánchez Valverde and the son of a mulatto slave girl.[5] With the aid of his father, Don Pablo, Báez's education was as good as any in the entire Spanish colony.[6] Don Pablo, a partisan of Juan Sánchez Ramírez, was a rich landowner who was eventually able to send young Buenaventura to France. Báez was no doubt greatly influenced by his French experiences.[7] On his return to Santo Domingo, Báez willingly served in the government of Boyer's Haitian occupation.[8] Moreover, he was an intimate of Boyer and believed in his philosophy.[9] Rather early in his career, Báez developed an ability to galvanize support for his actions. However, he was quite capable of changing course drastically if that seemed to be expedient.[10]

Even before Dominican independence, in 1843, Báez sought the protection of France, claiming to represent the majority of Dominicans.[11] Other protectionists of lesser importance who sought Spanish protection were Antonio López Villanueva, Padre Gaspar Hernández, and Pedro Pamíes. Francisco Pimentel was a protectionist who looked to England,[12] and Tomás Bobadilla contributed to Duarte's exile after independence.[13] Báez was far more adept than these men. The negotiations with France proved to be fruitful and in September 1843 the French consul to Haiti, Pierre Levasseur, heard the desires of protectionist Dominicans (among them Báez) for French affiliation. As a result of these meetings, a paper was released on 15 September 1843, directed to the French government, that detailed the terms under which France was to have sovereignty over Samaná and a governor in Santo Domingo City.[14]

So much were the French involved in the affairs of Santo Domingo at this time that some historians believe the capitulation of General Desgrotte on 27 February 1844 was due to the mediation of the French vice consul to Haiti, Juchereau de Saint Denys, and not because of evidence of overwhelming superiority of the Dominican revolutionaries.[15]

This mediation, however, was not offered in order to implement the foundation of an independent state but rather to set the stage for a French protectorate over Santo Domingo in the spirit of the 15 September 1843 resolution.[16]

The predictable Haitian response of retaliatory military action brought to the fore the powerful Dominican *caudillo* Pedro Santana, who had been turned into an ardent protectionist as a result of the influence of Saint Denys.[17] Known more as a "doer" than a thinker, Santana was also adept at political intrigue. He and his twin brother, Ramón, were born in Hincha on 29 June 1801, sons of Don Pedro and Doña Petronia Santana.[18] Young Pedro's parents were members

Pedro Santana.

of the country gentry and could afford Pedro some rudimentary education.[19] Haitian invasions eventually made it necessary for the Santanas to move to Seybo, where they became a slave-holding, land-owning family. Pedro and Ramón both grew up in an environment in which class distinctions were blurred due to the general impoverishment of the country and in which the belief of the necessity of outside help for the people of Santo Domingo was firmly fixed.[20] The elder Don Pedro had helped to lead the fight against the Frenchman Ferrand, but the conflict was not a fight for liberation as much as it was a struggle to deliver Santo Domingo to Spain.[21]

As a result of Don Pedro's heroics, the Santanas became one of the most respected families in Santo Domingo.[22] The Santana brothers, then only nine years old, were to benefit later from this fame.[23] Having grown up in an impoverished land that had been occupied by France, Spain, and Haiti, and having been the son of Ferrand's beheader,[24] by the time he was in his twenties, Pedro Santana was already exhibiting traits of brutishness and arrogance.[25] In 1826, young Pedro married Doña Micaela de Rivera, the widow of a Spanish captain who had fought with Sánchez Ramírez (his brother also married the widow's daughter).[26] When the widow's extensive holdings were passed on to him, Pedro refined his personality to make his forceful characteristics serve him well in management. He became accustomed to being a leader, giving orders, and never being crossed. His reputation as a tough, efficient, brutal *caudillo* spread throughout Seybo and beyond.[27] Although Santana's family was not greatly hurt by the Haitian occupation,[28] Pedro was known to have had anti-Haitian sentiments.[29] It was this attitude that caused Duarte to make the mistake of accepting Santana in the Dominican independence movement.[30]

Although he was a forceful general, Santana nevertheless knew how to use his energies. Called upon to resist the retaliations of the Haitians by the leaders of the newly established Dominican Republic, Santana initially held back because French representatives, backed by two war vessels, believed that the Haitians should be allowed to advance toward the capital, making the liberal members of the (Dominican) Junta Central more disposed to seek French protection.[31] Santana, now head of a large army, was in a position of strategic power, which he used greatly to his advantage when Duarte idealistically refused the Dominican presidency. On 12 July 1844, Santana, whose troops had "refused" to leave his side, marched into Santo Domingo City, declared himself ruler of the Republic, and sent his liberal rivals, including Sánchez, Mella, and Duarte, into prison and eventual exile.[32] The liberals were now all gone or dead. For more than thirty years to come, protectionism would be a cornerstone of Dominican foreign and domestic policy.

INSULAR POLITICS: HAITI AND ITS NEIGHBOR

At the time of the Dominican revolution, Haiti had economic, political, and racial problems. Its fiscal problems were worsened by its tenuous political position after independence. Lacerte states,

> Haiti was a major exporter of coffee in the first half of the nineteenth century and there were a number of foreign merchants already present in the country to purchase the crop. Instead of economic prosperity, the years after 1820 witnessed an economic decline which made the first black nation virtually ungovernable after 1843 save by the rule of *caudillos*. . . . There were many interrelated factors which brought about this situation, several of which were domestic problems, but all of which were exacerbated by the anomalous position in which Haiti found itself after the settlement at the Congress of Vienna. Up to 1815, the Napoleonic wars on the Continent had allowed the new nation to remain free of European pressures. The Treaty of Paris, however, changed all this. Under its stipulations, Louis XVIII was granted the right to regain all his American possessions. A secret article, agreed to by Great Britain, specifically recognized Haiti or Saint-Domingue as a French colony.[33]

Jean-Pierre Boyer's lack of understanding of the internal ills of the Haitian economy did little to help the situation.[34] The result was an increasingly impoverished and stagnant nation, its predicament directly related to the fear of foreign domination. Again, Lacerte:

> The potential threat of a renewal of French interest in her old colony had fashioned the earliest definition of Haitian nationalism. It was a unique expression of nationalism for this period since it was directed not only against France but against all white men. It was, thus, racist in nature but was not defined primarily as a black ideology. The Haitians drew up a series of laws designed to protect their country from outside intervention, which were largely successful in achieving this end, but which also slowed economic growth by the way in which they curtailed the activities of foreign merchants.[35]

The crowning blow was the huge indemnity demanded by France for recognition of Haitian independence in 1825.[36]

Haiti's troubles, however, did not stop with finances. The racial composition of its population presented still more difficulties. The world's greatest slave power, the United States, was only a few hundred miles away. Haiti's leaders—most notably Faustin Soulouque,

Table 1
Principal Encounters Won by Dominicans in Battles with Haitians

Battles	Dates	Site	Notable Dominicans
19th of March	19 March 1844	Azua	Antonio Duvergé Pedro Santana Felipe Alfau
30th of March	30 March 1844	Santiago	José María Imbert Archille Michell Fernando Valerio Francisco Caba Bartolo Mejía
Estrelleta	19 September 1845	Elías Piña	José Joachín Puello Valentín Alcántara Bernardino Pérez
Beller	27 October 1845	Dajabón	Antonio Salcedo Eugenio Pelletier José María López José María Imbert
El Número	17 April 1849	Baní	Antonio Duvergé
Las Carreras	21 April 1849	Baní	Pedro Santana
Santomé	22 December 1855	San Juan	José María Cabral
Cambronal	22 December 1855	Neiba	Francisco Sosa
Sabana Larga	24 October 1856	Dajabón	Juan Suero Juan Rodríguez

Source: Peguero and de los Santos, Visión General, 206.

who ruled from 1847 to 1859—were terrified that any non-Haitian (and particularly U.S.) presence on any part of the island of Hispaniola would lead to reenslavement.[37] Ironically, Haitian raids (to try to prevent this) only encouraged those Dominicans who actually wanted what Haiti did not: white representatives of a foreign presence on Dominican soil.[38]

THE INTERNATIONAL ARENA: THE DOMINICAN PAWN

It is ironic that the protectionists finally succeeded in eventually delivering the Dominican Republic to the power least capable of providing any adequate government, Spain.[39] Santana, Báez, and other protectionists had had a variety of powers from which to choose. The fact that Santana favored Spain (which eventually assumed formal control of the Dominican Republic in 1861) and that

Báez favored France matters less than the reality that the powers themselves had their own designs on the Dominican Republic. These plans existed not so much because of any intrinsic value that the Dominican Republic had (although Samaná was indeed a prize) but because at various times the Dominican Republic fit in with a particular foreign policy plan or statement.

Four major powers—Spain, France, Britain, and the United States—involved themselves deeply in the affairs of the Dominican Republic in the first years of independence. For Spain, the pleas of Santana for protection caused indifference until U.S. designs on Cuba warranted increased Spanish attention to Caribbean affairs, including the Dominican Republic.[40] By 1855 a commercial treaty was negotiated between the Dominican Republic and Spain. Soon Don Antonio María Segovia, consul general of Spain to the Dominican Republic, was able to use his considerable skills to help circumvent U.S. plans in the Caribbean.[41] The actual Spanish takeover of the Dominican Republic, which Santana credited himself with achieving through his own brand of diplomacy, was due at least as much to the desire of Spanish Prime Minister Leopold O'Donnell to achieve cohesion in Spain by directing attention to foreign exploits.[42]

The French were not as successful as Spain in colonizing the Dominican Republic, but they were not without designs—or influence. As we have seen, French assistance was pivotal in the actual struggle for Dominican independence. Moreover, even if they were to claim disinterest in the affairs of the Dominican Republic for the country's own sake, the French were heavily involved in the affairs of Haiti. Although the French were to respond erratically and mostly negatively to the numerous Dominican appeals for protection after 1844,[43] they helped the British assure Dominican independence because they realized that the Haitians could never pay the indemnity they owed France as long as they kept fighting Dominicans.[44] Moreover, at that time the British were dominating French foreign policy.[45] This was reflected by the assistance the French gave to the British attempts to stop the United States from establishing a territorial presence in the Dominican Republic.[46]

Unlike French policy, which was reactive and subject to the dictates of others, British and North American policy on the Dominican Republic and Hispaniola in general was aggressive, comprehensive, and linked to a larger global scheme. The British and the North Americans were engaged in a fight for supremacy on the seas and elsewhere. In the early to midnineteenth century Britain was the world's greatest maritime power; as such, it dreaded the rise of a strong U.S. presence in the Caribbean.[47] The British mounted a policy of antagonism to U.S. interests in strategic global theaters. Cuba and Hispaniola were part of a particularly sensitive area. British policy-maker Sir Stratford Canning, in the early part of the nine- teenth century, outlined a policy against U.S. expansionism that was continued by Viscount Palmerston.[48] Regarding U.S. expansionist desires in Cuba, Palmerston in 1857 stated:

> We are far away, weak from Distance, controlled by the indifference of the Nation . . . and by its Strong commercial interest in maintaining Peace with the United States. The result of this State of Things has been that we have given way Step by Step to the North Americans on every disputed matter, and I fear that we shall have more or less to do so upon almost every other Question except the maintenance of our own provinces and of our West Indian Islands—I have long felt inwardly convinced that the Anglo-Saxon Race will in (the) Process of Time become Masters of the whole American Continent North and South, by Reason of their superior Qualities as compared with the degenerate Spanish and Portuguese Americans; But whatever may be the effects of such a Result upon the interests of England, it is not for us to assist such a Consumation [sic] but on the contrary we ought to delay it as long as possible.[49]

Although Great Britain was the foremost imperialist power at that time, its actions in the Caribbean Basin were defensive—that is, Britain opposed U.S. territorial expansion in Cuba and Hispaniola. Britain did not want any new colonies in the area, preferring to promote stability in its existing possessions.[50] Its policy of aid to the Dominicans by mediation (as in the case of the famed Tripartite Intervention of 1851) was more a gesture to oblige the Haitians to desist attacking Dominicans and improve their part of the island.[51] The bulk of British energy, however, was spent in stopping North Americans from having any foothold in the Dominican Republic. They believed that the Spanish, already in debt to them and subject to encroachments from North Americans with designs on Cuba, needed help to hold on to their richest possession.[52] British zeal in their opposition to North American aims in Cuba probably made the French think, erroneously, that the British also had designs on Cuba. In fact, the French even appealed to the United States to deter the British.[53]

The United States of the 1840s and 1850s was under the legislative leadership of men favoring slavery and often expansion.[54] Though statesmen like Webster and later Seward probably acted out of a sense of duty and belief in the protection of North American interest,[55] others desired a fulfillment of the United States's "Manifest Destiny" (a term coined by magazine and newspaper editor John L. O'Sullivan[56]). After the election of President Franklin Pierce in 1852, expansionism and imperialism became administration policies. Pierce was the first president to proclaim territorial aggrandizement as an aim of an incoming administration.[57] "Young American" imperialism, sanctioned by Pierce, who favored proslavery appointees,[58] took many forms. One of these was the support of the intrigues of Soulé, Mason, and Buchanan in Europe, who demanded Cuba from Spain in what would be known as the Ostend Manifesto.[59] The Narciso López intrigues, in which López invaded Cuba three times, were encouraged by North Americans.[60] Filibustering, which had been revived in the 1840s, was rampant in the 1850s. This North American phenomenon, in which expansion was a cornerstone, was evident not only in annexationist sentiment ("Fifty-four-forty or Fight," for example), but also by the Pierce administration's largely overlooking the dark scandal in Nicaragua (a prelude to William Walker's eventual Nicaraguan dictatorship in 1856.)[61] According to Charles Brown, by the midnineteenth century not a year passed without U.S.-backed raids set afoot in Latin American countries.[62] Walker himself had a predilection for slavery, which seemingly reversed previous tendencies,[63] and firmly agreed with the dominant motivation of many filibusterers and expansionists: the desire to bring new slave states into the Union to maintain control of Congress and to create a vast slave empire.[64]

Reality for the Dominican Republic in the years following its independence, was bleak. The country was dominated by conservatives bent on obtaining foreign protection; it was adjoined by an unstable black nation that greatly feared reenslavement and that consequently mounted raids to reconquer the entire island; and it had the misfortune to have figured peripherally in the plans of several great powers, chief of which was the United States. Hispaniola's proximity to the United States, like that of Cuba's, certainly has been both a blessing and a bane. The flirtations that Dominicans were to have with annexation by the United States, discussed at more length in succeeding chapters, came directly from the weak status of the Dominican Republic as a nation.

NOTES

1. See William Javier Nelson, "Debt of Gratitude? British and French Circumvention of the Treaty of 1854 between the Dominican Republic and the United States," *Journal of Caribbean Studies* 6 (Autumn 1988): 275–85.

2. Betances de Pujadas, *Origen y Proyecciones*, 59.

3. Ibid.

4. Ibid., 68–69.

5. Monclús, *El Caudillismo*, 21.

6. Ibid., 22.

7. Emilio Rodríguez Demorizi, *Documentos para la Historia de la República Dominicana*, 3 vols. (Santo Domingo: Impresora Dominicana, 1959), 3:394–95.

8. Monclús, *El Caudillismo*, 22.

9. Ibid. Báez was said to have been "a man of the world in the worst sense of the phrase" by Rodman in *Quisqueya*, 61. Most of this narrative deals with the efforts of Báez, during most of 1868–71, to annex the Dominican Republic to the United States. Ironically, during an earlier presidency, Báez led a government noted for hostility against North Americans. See Tansill, *The United States and Santo Domingo*, 206–7.

10. According to one of the intimates of Charles Sumner, Báez was "the worst man living of whom he has any personal knowledge." See Charles Sumner, *Works of Charles Sumner*, 20 vols. (Boston: Lee and Shepard, 1883), 14:184.

11. Betances de Pujadas, *Origen y Proyecciones*, 69.

12. Ibid., 69–71. See also Victor Garrido, *Política de Francia en Santo Domingo, 1844–1846* (Santo Domingo: Editora del Caribe, 1962), 20–21.

13. Welles, *Naboth's Vineyard*, 1:68.

14. Betances de Pujadas, *Origen y Proyecciones*, 69.

15. Ibid., 72; Tansill, *The United States and Santo Domingo*, 124n.

16. Betances de Pujadas, *Origen y Proyecciones*, 72.

17. Ibid., 73–74; Welles, *Naboth's Vineyard*, 1:68–69.

18. Juan Daniel Balcácer, *Pedro Santana: Historia Política de un Déspota* (Santo Domingo: Editora Taller, 1974), 25; Emilio Rodríguez Demorizi, in *Papeles de General Santana* (Rome: Stab. Tipográfico, 1952), asserted that Santana was born in 1800.

19. Balcácer, *Pedro Santana*, 25; Monclús, *El Caudillismo*.

20. Balcácer, *Pedro Santana*, 30.

21. Ibid., 33–34.

22. Ibid.

23. Ibid.

24. Ibid., 39; Welles, *Naboth's Vineyard*, 1:43–44.

25. Balcácer, *Pedro Santana*, 39; see also Emilio Rodríguez Demorizi, *Santana y los Poetas de su Tiempo* (Santo Domingo: Editora del Caribe, 1969).

26. Balcácer, *Pedro Santana*, 47.

27. Ibid.

28. Ibid., 48.

29. Ibid.

30. Ibid.

31. Welles, *Naboth's Vineyard*, 1:68.

32. Ibid., p. 70.

33. Lacerte, "Xenophobia and Economic Decline," 499–500.

34. Heinl and Heinl, *Written in Blood*, 172–79.

35. Lacerte, "Xenophobia and Economic Decline," 500.

36. Fagg, *Cuba, Haiti and the Dominican Republic*, 125.

37. Logan, *Haiti and the Dominican Republic*, 34.

38. Nelson, "The Haitian Political Situation," 235.

39. Welles, *Naboth's Vineyard*, 1:190–211, describes in detail how Santana cleverly succeeded in delivering the Dominican Republic to Spain, the only instance in the history of the western hemisphere of a colony "voluntarily" returning to the metropole.

40. Ibid., 163; See also H. Butler Clarke, *Modern Spain, 1815–1898* (New York: A.M.S. Press, 1969), 250–76.

41. Welles, *Naboth's Vineyard*, 1:163–73.

42. Martin A. S. Hume, *Modern Spain, 1788–1898* (New York: G. P. Putnam's Sons, 1909), 440, 446. See also Raymond Carr, *Spain 1808–1975*, 2d ed. (Oxford: Clarendon Press, 1982), 260. For a look at O'Donnell's relationship with the Spanish head of state, Isabel II, see Elizabeth Wormeley Latimer, *Spain in the Nineteenth Century* (Chicago: A. C. McClurg and Co., 1898), 313. For an appreciation of the character of Spanish politics in the nineteenth century, see E. Ramón Arango, *The Spanish Political System: Franco's Legacy* (Boulder, Colo.: Westview Press, 1978), 18–19ff.

43. Welles, *Naboth's Vineyard*, 1:81–98.

44. Heinl and Heinl, *Written in Blood*, 208; see also Welles, *Naboth's Vineyard*, 1:112.

45. Charles Brown, *Agents of Manifest Destiny* (Chapel Hill: University of North Carolina Press, 1980), 126; Lawrence C. Jennings, *France and Europe in 1848: A Study of French Foreign Affairs in Time of Crisis* (London: Oxford University Press, 1973), 6, 242; John B. Wolf, *France: 1815 to the Present* (New York: Prentice-Hall, 1940), 158. See also Welles, *Naboth's Vineyard*, 1:102, and Tansill, *The United States and Santo Domingo*, 124n.

46. Nelson, "Debt of Gratitude," 281.

47. H. C. Allen, *Great Britain and the United States: A History of Anglo-American Relations* (New York: St. Martin's Press, 1955), 369. See also Tansill, *The United States and Santo Domingo*, 182.

48. Allen, *Great Britain and the United States*, 423.

49. R. W. Van Alstyne, "Anglo-American Relations 1853–1857," *American Historical Review* 42 (1937): 500.

50. Allen, *Great Britain and the United States*, 369.

51. Welles, *Naboth's Vineyard*, 1:112.

52. As it turned out, this was prophetic, since almost fifty years later the Spanish-Cuban-American War resulted in the loss of Cuba and the hegemony of the United States over that nation in the years that followed.

53. Jennings, *France and Europe*, 242.

54. So complete was the domination of the southern states in the United States Congress that it held off from recognizing the Dominican Republic because it could not find enough "white" Dominicans. See William Ray Manning, comp., *Diplomatic Correspondence of the United States: Inter-American Affairs, 1831–1860*, 12 vols. (Washington, D.C.: Carnegie Endowment for International Peace, 1932–39), 6:55–60.

55. Welles, *Naboth's Vineyard*, 1:316, describes Seward's motivations. For a look at Welles's impressions of Daniel Webster, see 112–13, 141.

56. Brown, *Agents of Manifest Destiny*, 16.

57. Ibid., 109; Logan, *Haiti and the Dominican Republic*, 37, and Welles, *Naboth's Vineyard*, 1:146, also noted Pierce's expansionist tendencies. Selden Rodman, in *Quisqueya*, 66–67, gives some background (e.g., Pierce's service in the Mexican War and his actions in the successful Gadsden Purchase) into Pierce's motivations. See also Pérez y Pérez, *Historia Diplomática*, 279.

58. Pérez y Pérez, *Historia Diplomática*, 279.

59. Brown, *Agents of Manifest Destiny*, 140–41.

60. Bailey and Nasatir, *Latin America*, 655; see also Fagg, *Cuba, Haiti and the Dominican Republic*, 35.

61. Brown, *Agents of Manifest Destiny*, 355, has some interesting material concerning Walker's relation to the slave states. For a look at Walker's fantastic career, see 337–58; see also Bailey and Nasatir, *Latin America*, 631–32. Welles, *Naboth's Vineyard*, 1:138, shows the avaricious nature of U.S. Latin American policy in its response to Walker's intrigues.

62. Brown, *Agents of Manifest Destiny*, 3.

63. Ibid., 337–58.

64. Ibid., 115; Tansill, *The United States and Santo Domingo*, 184; Allen, *Great Britain and the United States*, 423.

4

Prelude to Dominican Annexation

Cuando la hormiga se quiere perder, alas le quieren nacer

(He who looks for trouble finds what he seeks.)

—Dominican proverb

In 1865 both the United States and the Dominican Republic had ended savage wars. The U.S. Civil War, the most deadly and destructive in that nation's history,[1] had served to paralyze the South while enriching the North.[2] The level of devastation in the Dominican Republic, however, probably exceeded that of the United States.

The Dominican Republic had just defeated the Spanish, permanently driving them out and ending an astonishing four years in which they went to war to remove a foreign presence they had requested in 1861.[3] Thus they became people who had to fight for their independence twice. In all fairness, one should note that it was Pedro Santana who did the asking, not the long-suffering Dominican people, who were never consulted on political decisions.[4] The fratricidal War of Restoration (so called because Santana, a Dominican, fought for the Spanish against the independence fighters) produced some Dominican generals later considered as heroes, such as Gregorio Luperón,[5] and resulted in the death of Santana.[6] In reality, however, the end of the war signaled a return to the days of weakness, guile, avarice, and strife that had marked the young republic from 1844 to 1861.

Before the Spanish occupation, Santana and Buenaventura Báez had alternated in the presidency, Santana holding office three times and Báez twice.[7] The Dominican Republic had made little, if any, economic progress from 1844 to 1861.[8] The general population had come no closer to any meaningful participation in political life[9] and the activities of the various Dominican presidents had consisted mostly of dealing with the ever-present Haitian threat, trying to become rich at public expense, and jockeying to affiliate the country with various foreign powers.[10] At times, the self-serving nature of Dominican presidents during this period had assumed comic proportions. Consider the following description of President Manuel Jiménez, who had served as president from September 1848 to May 1849:

> His whole time was spent in cleaning, training and fighting cocks, it being frequently necessary to send acts of Congress and other official papers to the cock-pit for his approval and signature. Under his rule, everything fell into confusion, which state of things was soon made known to Soulouque and incited him to the invasion [of the Republic].[11]

The Haitians, who in 1844 and 1849–50 had mounted full-scale invasions immediately after independence, had succeeded in sacking and looting those parts of the country with which their armies had come into contact, placing the Dominican people in an almost constant state of emergency and providing a rationale by which both Santana and Báez were to try to annex or affiliate their country to a foreign power.[12] Aside from Spain, which was aided in its 1861 takeover of the Dominican Republic by the fact the United States was involved in its own North-South conflict,[13] European interest in the Dominican Republic had been confined during this period mostly to thwarting the designs of North Americans with regard to establishing a presence there[14] and encouraging the Haitians to desist from attacking it.[15]

North American involvement, however, had been significant after 1846. Although the Dominicans had not been disposed to seek North American assistance,[16] immediately after independence this attitude had quickly changed in the face of the continued Haitian menace and the seeming indifference of European powers.[17] As early as 6 January 1845, Dr. José M. Caminero, special Dominican envoy to the United States, had been received by U.S. Secretary of State John C. Calhoun.[18] As a result of growing North American interest in the Dominican Republic, young naval Lieutenant David D. Porter had been sent there in May of 1846.[19] With difficulty, Porter had managed to travel to various parts of the Dominican Republic and had reported, among other things, the utility of Samaná Bay as a naval base.[20]

This small notation was to have a great deal of significance in Dominican affairs in succeeding years since Samaná was to become a focal point for Dominican–North American negotiations regarding a North American presence in the Dominican Republic. In 1854 discussions between the Dominican government of Pedro Santana and the United States had nearly resulted in the establishment of a U.S.

naval station on Samaná Bay,[21] helping to cause yet another Haitian invasion.[22] Alarm over U.S. activity in the Dominican Republic had, in fact, indirectly led to the Spanish occupation from 1861 to 1865.

Like the European powers, the United States had an assortment of people with differing motives within the ranks of those favoring an increased American presence in the Dominican Republic. Some, like President Franklin Pierce and then envoy James Buchanan, had been ardent imperialists who favored expansion. To them the Dominican Republic—as well as Cuba—represented a symbol of empire.[23] Others, like Secretary of State Daniel Webster, had been genuinely concerned with the protection of North American interests in the Caribbean Basin thought to be threatened by European powers.[24] Still others, however, had seen the Dominican Republic as just another arena in which to exploit the gullible. To be sure, they had been often joined by equally conniving Dominican politicians. Santana and Báez had been quite adept at not only utilizing the sympathies of their fellow Dominicans, but also at pitting one foreign power against another to gain the best advantage.[25]

Like the Dominican protectionists, the group of Americans wanting to advance selfish aims by securing a U.S. presence in the Dominican Republic had a few members who were more active than others. Among the most active from 1854 until 1871 were General William L. Cazneau and, later, his associate Colonel Joseph W. Fabens. It was Cazneau, as special agent to the Dominican Republic, who had so encouraged U.S. Secretary of State Marcy and who was behind the failed efforts to establish a U.S. naval base on Samaná in 1854.[26] These efforts, jointly fostered by Pedro Santana, had every indication of ultimate success but had been foiled by special circumstances. These included the activities of then Captain George B. McClellan, who had disregarded the wishes of the Dominican Congress by prematurely surveying Samaná, and the skillful use of North American racism by the British and French, who had warned the Dominicans that U.S. presence on Dominican territory would result in the eventual enslavement of all "negroes."[27]

"General" William L. Cazneau, born in Fort Hill, Boston, of French Roman Catholic ancestry, was the son of a Salem, Massachusetts, man.[28] Lured by the promise of high adventure and financial gain he later went to Texas and participated in the struggle against Mexico that ultimately resulted in the annexation of Texas. As a result of his activities Cazneau was called "General" but his career in Texas was cut short in 1853.[29] During his years of adventuring on the Mexican frontier Cazneau had learned Spanish and the art of armed infiltration.[30] Failing in his bid to arrange the U.S. takeover of Samaná Bay, Cazneau "retired" to his Dominican estate, "Estancia Esmeralda," near Santo Domingo City and waited for his next opportunity.[31] This opportunity was not to come with his next appointment as special agent in 1859: the Spaniards were about to take over and the United States was heading inexorably toward civil war.[32] However, Cazneau and his newfound associate Joseph W. Fabens had set out to diversify their approach to taking advantage of the riches of the Dominican Republic soon after the Spanish takeover. Fabens was by chance also a native of Boston who had gone to Texas.[33] He was the author of several books and was reputed to have been involved in the use of camels in the North American Southwest, a creative idea that was initially effective but caused so much panic that it was scrapped.[34]

On 1 October 1862 Cazneau and Fabens organized the "American West India Company."[35] What makes this business remarkable is that it had been established to promote North American settlement in the Dominican Republic, which was now nominally part of Spain. Apparently Cazneau had been able to overcome his previous reservations about such an enterprise.[36] By issuing statements describing the "undeveloped riches" of the Dominican Republic, Cazneau and Fabens had managed to convince a number of North American settlers to locate there.[37] The transparency of this misinformation is obvious in the following quotations:

[Some twelve or fifteen American settlers had recently arrived in the Dominican Republic under the auspices of] Col. J. W. Fabens (of Greytown Fame), and William L. Cazneau (former United States especial agent of this city). They all intend to return to the United States by the first conveyance, cursing in their hearts the "West India Company" of Fabens and Cazneau, and more particularly the Spaniards in St. Domingo.[38]

Further:

[Of the last lot of emigrants sent out by the West India Company, some fourteen in all, nine had died,] two went home, and the rest with those who came before are down with the fever and not expected to live.[39]

While Cazneau's efforts on behalf of Dominican settlement were going on, he had not lost sight of the revolution taking place elsewhere in the Dominican Republic. The Spaniards had been outdoing themselves in the *España Boba* tradition (ineffective government) and insurrection was afoot. Pedro Santana, dying as a "Spaniard" and not a Dominican, would go down in history as a

William Henry Seward. *(Courtesy of Perkins Library, Duke University.)*

traitor. Judging that this ex-colony was not worth the trouble, the last of the Spanish forces had sailed away in July 1865.[40]

For Cazneau, this era of postwar devastation indicated need for a new plan of action. This new strategy was a rewording of one of his earlier plans to promote the establishment of a free trade zone on the island of Hispaniola. He had advocated this idea in 1859–60 but it was jettisoned as a result of both the U.S. Civil War and the Spanish occupation.[41] For this project Cazneau enlisted the considerable skills of his wife, Jane McManus Cazneau. The author of several books, including a description of the descendants of the North American blacks in Samaná,[42] Jane Cazneau wrote to the U.S. Secretary of the Interior, James Harlan, to urge him to consider the arrangement that her husband had suggested some years earlier.[43] Although the entire letter is too lengthy to be reproduced here, the following passage is significant:

> . . . 1. In consideration of amity, recognition, etc., the Dominican Republic would cede to the United States a naval station on the Bay of Manzanill at the northwest corner of her limits—the Bay to be made neutral of war forever to all nations. . . .[44]

After concluding this letter with the assertion that the Dominican government would be able to accede to this proposal "at once," she requested the letter to be forwarded to U.S. Secretary of State William H. Seward.[45] This was to have immense significance because Seward at that time was genuinely interested in a naval base in the Caribbean.[46] Moreover, freed from the bondage of internal war, the United States could now aspire to the hemispheric leadership that it "deserved"—as reflected in the speeches of President Andrew Johnson.[47] In all fairness, one should point out that Seward was probably motivated by a patriotic concern with European encroachment in the Caribbean and a desire to maintain a strategically viable naval strength in that region.[48] Whatever Seward's motives, however, Cazneau lost no time in capitalizing on them. When Seward decided to visit Santo Domingo City on 14 January 1866 to get first hand information concerning the Dominican Republic, Cazneau was there:

> Mr. Cazneau was on the watch, and managed to get him [Seward] to his house before I or any other citizen of the United States knew of his arrival. His motives in his cunning management to have him quite to himself were readily understood. Having always publicly vilified and traduced him, it would not suit him to have any one else present in his conferences with him. As Mr. Seward was in the city but a few hours, he succeeded in preventing any other citizen seeing him.[49]

Partly as a result of Cazneau's enthusiasm, Seward would toy with the idea of a naval base—not at Manzanillo, but at Samaná—for two more years.

During this time, what had the Dominicans been doing? The vast majority of Dominicans simply had been trying to stay alive. While fighting the Spaniards, Dominican insurgents destroyed village and town so as to deny their use to Spanish troops.[50] For other Dominicans of better means, however, the presidency remained a valuable prize by which one could manipulate public offices and funds.[51] Thus all the ingredients were present to ensure that the sorry state of Dominican politics would not change. The population as a whole had made little economic or educational progress: any improvements that had come were lost in the Second War of Independence.[52] Some of the same politicians (such as Buenaventura Báez) still sought office, some new ones (like José María Cabral) had arrived, and Cazneau and Fabens were now constantly on hand to "advise" embattled Dominican leaders.

Since the Haitians' final serious invasion of the Dominican Republic had been in late 1855, an observer might wonder what threat could face a Dominican president. While it was true that the Dominican Republic had less to fear from Haiti than before the Spanish occupation, the adjoining nation nevertheless made a convenient staging area from which to mount revolutions against an incumbent president.[53] Moreover, a great many Haitians still intensely feared the United States, which made any Dominican president's overture to the North Americans a reason for helping a revolutionary leader to remove that president.[54] Last, the democratic concepts of referendum and consensus were foreign to an uneducated Dominican nation that was led mostly by generals or political speculators. When Pedro Santana had delivered the Dominican Republic to Spain, he explained to a Spaniard in Santo Domingo City why he was not expecting any initial opposition: "I have made you an immensely valuable gift, for I have given you a people without journalists and devoid of lawyers."[55]

In this atmosphere, speculators like Cazneau and Fabens were bound to flourish, particularly when they had the additional advantage of presenting their "information" from the Dominican Republic to North Americans who were often long distances away and/or had little knowledge of the Spanish language or Dominican culture. The ability of Cazneau to harmonize his desires with the aims of various Dominican leaders whom he advised can be gleaned from the following comments. The first came in 1859, when Báez and Cazneau were politically opposed to each other:

France, England and Spain still continue their support of Báez and his party, whose aim is to place power in the hands of the Negroes; if successful the whites will be dispossessed of their property, citizenship and perhaps their lives and lead to the annexation of Dominica to Hayti.[56]

Still later, when he was actively working with Báez to annex the Dominican Republic to the United States, the general had this to say about his former nemesis:

[Báez, who was soon to be inaugurated as President of the Dominican Republic, would] welcome and encourage American enterprises of every description. Knowing as I do, that this island possesses a great gold bearing territory which the introduction of American skill and capital is sure to develop speedily, I am fully convinced that if the negotiation above alluded to is carried out with Mr. Báez, *and the protection of our flag extended over any portion of this country,* it will not only be hailed with joy and gratitude here, but will give to our country a new and extended field for enterprises, and a very prolific source of national wealth.[57]

Hidden in this passage is the reason why Cazneau exerted so much effort in 1854 for a simple naval base. For several reasons the negotiations with Seward for a naval base at Samaná had gone for naught by 1868. First, the Dominican Congress still had not been completely corrupted, as it would be by Báez. An article in the Dominican constitution expressly forbade any alienation of the national territory (thus prohibiting an outright sale of Samaná).[58] The Dominican Congress still had some persons who took the constitution seriously. Second, President José María Cabral's very negotiations with the North Americans were a cause for a revolution against him. When details had been finally worked out for a lease (as opposed to a sale) of Samaná, Cabral's government promptly fell from power by January 1868.[59]

The beneficiary of this change in Dominican government was Buenaventura Báez, who was back for another term of service as his country's chief executive. Báez, as the reader will recall, was quite active in negotiating with France for a French protectorate over Santo Domingo and was a veteran of the intrigues of Dominican politics.[60] He had, in fact, held office immediately after the second independence, only to lose it for reasons quite typical of both Báez and Dominican politics in general, his enemies having claimed that he used the presidency for his individual interest.[61] This time Báez was determined to avoid a similar fate, which he judged could happen only if he were to attain a closer association with the United States. Tansill describes it thusly:

It is very likely, of course, that this friendly disposition was partly induced by the efforts of that choice pair of American imperialists, Colonel Fabens and General Cazneau. Despite the swiftly changing fortunes of the Dominican Republic, these adventurers had retained an invincible belief in the rich opportunities that awaited American development. They soon discovered in President Báez a kindred spirit who regarded patriotism in terms of pecuniary profits, and they made haste to form an unholy trinity that had few qualms as to how low they might have to stoop to conquer.[62]

That alliance having been established, the three looked again to Seward, dangling before him the prize of Samaná. Seward, however, mainly motivated by a desire for a Caribbean (not necessarily Dominican) naval base, was not as eager for a purchase or lease of Samaná, partly due to State Department difficulties such as the negative effects of the purchase of Alaska in 1867.[63] In spite of Seward's hesitance, the trio found it increasingly difficult to give up.[64]

In July 1868, the Dominican government, aided by some behind-the-scenes maneuvering by Fabens, decided to appeal to the U.S. Secretary of State for annexation.[65] Báez soon succeeded in causing the sending of a significant despatch from the U.S. Commercial Agent in the Dominican Republic to Seward in the autumn of 1868. In this communication Seward was told that the Dominican president wished to place his country under the protection of the United States. This action, Seward was told, would give the country more stability in the face of the overthrowing of the monarchy in Spain and the subsequent possible immigration of a great number of Spaniards from Cuba and Puerto Rico.[66]

Clearly Báez had known what would arouse apprehension on the part of Seward. Seward always feared a repeated attempt by European powers to infringe upon the Monroe Doctrine. An admonition that Spaniards might descend upon the Dominican Republic en masse was enough to alarm Seward of foreign intrigue in the Caribbean.[67] Moreover, owing to the difficulties in the U.S. Senate with the treaty for the purchase of the Danish West Indies, Seward had still failed to obtain what he most wanted: a coaling station in the West Indies.[68] These disappointments helped to overcome Seward's earlier worry about involvement in the Dominican Republic, and he therefore gave full support to the idea of Dominican annexation. President Andrew Johnson, who had few qualms himself about the concept of a stronger U.S. influence in the Caribbean, was quickly won over to the idea of annexation and delivered the following passage in his fourth annual message to Congress on 9 December 1868:

It can not be long before it will become necesssary for this Government to lend some effective aid to the solution of the political and social problems which are continually kept before the world by the two republics of the island of St. Domingo, and which are now disclosing themselves more distinctly than heretofore in the island of Cuba. The subject is recommended to your consideration with all the more earnestness becaușe I am satisfied that the time has arrived when even so direct a proceeding as a proposition for an annexation of the two Republics of the island of St. Domingo would not only receive the consent of the people interested, but would also give satisfaction to all other foreign nations.[69]

For the next two and a half years, the fate of the Dominican Republic as an independent nation would hang in the balance. The process of annexation had begun.

Notes

1. Richard N. Current et al., *The Essentials of American History,* 2d ed. (New York: Alfred A. Knopf, 1976), 153, 166.

2. Ibid. See also Allen Weinstein and R. Jackson Wilson, *Freedom and Crisis,* 2 vols. (New York: Random House, 1974), 1:415–16.

3. Welles, *Naboth's Vineyard,* 1:190–91ff.

4. Ibid., 223–24.

5. For information on Luperón's life, see Manuel Rodríguez Objío, *Gregorio Luperón e Historia de la Restauración* (Santiago: Editorial el Diario, 1939); see also Emilio Rodríguez Demorizi, *Luperón y Hostos* (Santo Domingo: Editora Montalvo, 1939) and Luperón's own autobiography, *Notas Autobiográficas y Apuntes Historicos* (reprint, Santo Domingo: Editora de Santo Domingo, 1974).

6. Rodman, *Quisqueya,* 81; Welles, *Naboth's Vineyard,* 1:270–71. Also see Pedro M. Archambault, *Historia de la Restauración,* 2d ed. (Santo Domingo: Ediciones de Taller, 1973), chap. 21.

7. Logan, *Haiti and the Dominican Republic,* 203–4.

8. Franklin J. Franco Pichardo, *La República Dominicana: Clases, Crisis y Comandos* (Havana: Casa de las Américas, 1966), 11–14.

9. Welles, *Naboth's Vineyard,* 1:224; Rodman, *Quisqueya,* 76.

10. Rodman, *Quisqueya,* 62, 65.

11. Benjamin E. Green to John M. Clayton, 27 September 1849, Vol. 15, 4 June 1847–47–August 1850, Despatches from Special Agents to the Department of State, National Archives and Records Service, GSA, Washington, D.C.; Microform Number M37/Roll Number 15.

12. Welles, *Naboth's Vineyard,* 1:105–6, 136.

13. Tansill, *The United States and Santo Domingo,* 213–15.

14. The British and French were also interested in thwarting each other, which may have explained why neither managed to establish any type of hold on Dominican territory. See Welles, *Naboth's Vineyard,* 1:103, and Jennings, *France and Europe,* 242.

15. Nelson, "Debt of Gratitude."

16. Tansill, *The United States and Santo Domingo,* 124.

17. Ibid., 125.

18. Ibid.

19. Ibid., 127.

20. Papers of David D. Porter, Perkins Library, Duke University.

21. Nelson, "Debt of Gratitude," 278–81.

22. Welles, *Naboth's Vineyard*, 1:156; Rodman, *Quisqueya*, 67.

23. Nelson, "Debt of Gratitude." See also Current et al., *The Essentials*, 142.

24. Welles, *Naboth's Vineyard*, 1:112–16.

25. For a look at both how Báez manipulated U.S. interest to pressure France for protection and how Santana did the same to successfully gain the protection of Spain, see ibid., 102 and 190–91ff.

26. Ibid., 137; see also Nelson, "Debt of Gratitude" and Pérez y Pérez, *Historia Diplomática*, 227–86.

27. Pérez y Pérez, *Historia Diplomática*, 277–86.

28. Melvin Knight, *The Americans in Santo Domingo* (New York: Vanguard Press, 1928), 6. See also *Report of the U.S. Senate Select Committee on the Memorial of Davis Hatch*, Senate Report No. 234, 41st Cong., 2d sess., 178. Hereafter cited as *Hatch Report*.

29. Welles, *Naboth's Vineyard*, 1:136–37.

30. Knight, *The Americans*, 6.

31. Welles, *Naboth's Vineyard*, 1:154–55.

32. Tansill, *The United States and Santo Domingo*, 208–12.

33. Ibid., 344.

34. Joseph W. Fabens, "The Uses of the Camel: Considered with a View to His Introduction into Our Western States and Territories" (paper presented at the annual meeting of the American Geographical and Statistical Society, New York, 2 March 1865). See also Maurice Matloff, gen. ed., *American Military History* (Washington, D.C.: Office of Chief of Military History, 1969), 180.

35. Tansill, *The United States and Santo Domingo*, 216.

36. The following quote from Rodman (*Quisqueya*, 74–75) is illustrative: "Probably nothing less than the imminence of [the] Civil War at home prevented Buchanan from acting upon this and more urgent pleas for intervention. Cazneau had commercial interests in Santo Domingo to protect, and as he realized which way the wind was blowing, he began to minimize Santana's negotiations with Spain in his reports to Washington, at the same time going out of his way to blacken the reputation of Jonathan Elliott, the American commercial agent, whom he accused of both drunkenness and 'incitement of the colored class against the government.' It was no wonder that Santana's foes could make small headway."

37. Tansill, *The United States and Santo Domingo*, 217–19.

38. William G. Jaeger to William H. Seward, 6 April 1863, vol. 4, 2 January 1861–10 January 1864, Despatches from United States Consuls in Santo Domingo 1837–1906, National Archives and Records Service, GSA, Washington, D.C., T 56/Roll 4.

39. Ibid., 2 July 1863.

40. The Spanish had grown tired of O'Donnell's brand of imperialism. When he fell, the bottom fell out of the Santo Domingo initiative. See Rodman, *Quisqueya*, 81–82.

41. Tansill, *The United States and Santo Domingo*, 208–12.

42. See Jane McManus Cazneau, *Our Winter Eden: Pen Pictures of the Tropics* (New York: The Authors Publishing Co., 1878).

43. Tansill, *The United States and Santo Domingo*, 224–25.

44. Cora Montgomery Cazneau to James Harlan, 6 September 1865, William H.

Seward Papers, Department of Rare Books and Manuscripts, Rush Rhees Library, University of Rochester, Rochester, New York.

45. Tansill, *The United States and Santo Domingo*, 225.

46. Ibid., 234–35, 245.

47. Tulio M. Cestero, *Estados Unidos y las Antillas* (Madrid: Compañía Ibero-Americana de Publicaciones, 1931), 17. Abraham Lincoln also was preoccupied with expansion and national security. See William Appleman Williams, *Empire as a Way of Life* (New York: Oxford University Press, 1980), 92–93, and Ernest N. Paolino, *The Foundations of the American Empire: William Henry Seward and U.S. Foreign Policy* (Ithaca, N.Y.: Cornell University Press, 1973), 17.

48. Welles, *Naboth's Vineyard*, 1:354. William H. Seward's desires for overseas expansion were part of a coherent plan. His aims were multidimensional. Interested in national security and U.S.-commercial expansion, he saw Great Britain as the United States's true rival for domination. His foreign policy goals in Asia were linked to opening up new markets for American capitalism. Seward posited that in general Latin American republics, because of their degenerate state, would eventually become a part of the United States. With regard to the Caribbean specifically, Seward was defensive, as a safeguard against foreign attacks. As secretary of state under Lincoln, he had countenanced foreign interference and knew that England and France had colonies in the Caribbean from which they could mount attacks. See Paolino, *Foundations*, 32, and Frederick Merk, *Manifest Destiny and Mission in American History* (New York: Alfred A. Knopf, 1963), 229; Charles Callan Tansill, *The Purchase of the Danish West Indies* (Baltimore, The Johns Hopkins Press, 1932), 1; George E. Baker, *The Works of William H. Seward*, 5 vols. (New York: Redfield, and Boston: Houghton Mifflin and Co., 1853–84), 4:331ff. I must also add that although Seward was justly considered an expansionist, the United States had certain legitimate prerogatives beyond those espoused by Seward. For example, the country was undergoing a rapid westward expansion that necessitated a faster and more convenient route west. This resulted in attention on an isthmus crossing that would in turn call for a naval defense of this canal/crossing. European fear of an American canal/crossing was reflected in the Clayton-Bulwer Treaty of 1850. See Ludwell Lee Montague, *Haiti and the United States, 1714–1938* (Durham, N.C.: Duke University Press, 1940).

49. *Hatch Report*, 126.

50. William G. Jeager to Steward, 18 April 1864, vol. 5, 18 January 1864–19 December 1868, Despatches from U.S. Consuls, T 56/Roll 5. See also Rodman, *Quisqueya*, 82, and Welles, *Naboth's Vineyard*, 1:242.

51. Tansill, *The United States and Santo Domingo*, 231; see also Cladio Vedovato, *Politics, Foreign Trade and Economic Development: A Study of the Dominican Republic* (New York: St. Martin's Press, 1986), 21–22.

52. Logan, *Haiti and the Dominican Republic*, 42; also Juan Isidro Jiménez Grullón, *La República Dominicana: Una Ficción* (Mérida, Venezuela: Talleres Gráficos Universitarios, 1965), 151–52.

53. Welles, *Naboth's Vineyard*, 1:345, 361, 387, 401.

54. Ibid., 394; see also Rodman, *Quisqueya*, 85.

55. Rodman, *Quisqueya*, 76; Welles, *Naboth's Vineyard*, 1:224.

56. William L. Cazneau to William L. Marcy, 2 July 1859, vol. 19, 20 February 1852–1 July 1861, Communications Received by the Department of State from Special Agents of the Department of State, 1794–1906. National Archives and Records Service, GSA, Washington, D.C., M 37/Roll 9.

57. Cazneau to Seward, 18 April 1868, vol. 2, 11 January 1869–17 July 1871,

Notes from the Legations of the Dominican Republic in the United States to the Department of State, 1844–1906, National Archives and Records Service, GSA, Washington, D.C., T 801/Roll 1. Italics added.

58. Tansill, *The United States and Santo Domingo*, 241.

59. Welles, *Naboth's Vineyard*, 1 : 339–40.

60. Logan, *Haiti and the Dominican Republic*, 203–4, lists all Dominican presidents up to Joaquín Balaguer's election in 1966. Báez's return to power was facilitated financially by the Jesurún Merchant House of Curaçao. This merchant house was also the principal Dutch money lender to the Venezuelan government. See C.Ch. Goslinga, *Curaçao and Guzmán Blanco: A Case Study of Small Power Politics in the Caribbean* (The Hague: Martinus Nijhoff, 1975), 31, 34. See also Fabens to Fish, 1 April 1869, vol. 2, Notes from the Legations, T 801/Roll 1. For a candid description of Sylvain Salnave's and Báez's aid to help each other gain the Haitian and Dominican presidencies, respectively, see Montague, *Haiti and the United States*, 91–92. See also Arthur Folsom to Seward, 24 May 1866, vol. 9, 25 January 1858–13 December 1866, Despatches from United States Consuls in Cap Haitien 1797–1906, National Archives and Records Services, GSA, Washington, D.C., M 9/Roll 9.

61. Tansill, *The United States and Santo Domingo*, 230–31.

62. Ibid., 258.

63. Ibid., 262. Seward's long, unsuccessful struggle to have the 24 October 1867 treaty for the purchase of the Virgin Islands ratified by the U.S. Congress is described in Tansill, *The Purchase*, chap. 2. For another professional view of the Virgin Islands' strategic military value to the United States, see James Parton, *Danish Islands: Are We Bound in Honor to Pay for Them?* (Boston: Fields, Osgood and Co., 1869), appendix. The book as a whole is in favor of the acquisition of the Virgin Islands. Not only was Seward desirous of a Caribbean naval base, but he was also in favor of the acquisition of Cuba and Puerto Rico. See Merk, *Manifest Destiny*, p. 229.

64. Welles, *Naboth's Vineyard*, 1 : 343–44.

65. Tansill, *The United States and Santo Domingo*, 267.

66. Welles, *Naboth's Vineyard*, 1 : 349–50.

67. Ibid., 347.

68. Ibid., 353–54.

69. James D. Richardson, *Messages and Papers of Presidents, 1789–1897*, 10 vols. (Washington, D.C.: Government Printing Office, 1896–99), 6 : 689. Seward was influential here. The following quote from Logan, *Haiti and the Dominican Republic*, 44, is significant: "The rejection by the Senate of the treaty for the purchase of the Danish West Indies had led Seward, who almost certainly drafted this part of the annual message, to a disingenuous statement which shocked his former associates in the cause of Abolition."

5

Grant and Annexation

Dime con quien andas y te diré quien eres.

(A man is known by the company he keeps.)

—Dominican proverb

The near-miss of Dominican annexation was chiefly a story of bungled efforts by Cazneau, Fabens, Báez, and their supporters, including President Ulysses S. Grant of the United States. Initially it was not a case of a popular uprising in the Dominican Republic smashing the designs of Báez. It was also not the result of a groundswell of indignation in the United States thwarting the plans of the proannexationists. The truth of the matter was that then, as well as now, the Dominican Republic never occupied much attention in the minds of the U.S. body politic. John Fagg has stated,

> To the United States this country [the Dominican Republic] has posed occasional problems but has never absorbed much attention. Washington was slow to recognize its independence and was not particularly alarmed when Spanish control was restored during the Civil War. Presidents Andrew Johnson, Grant and Benjamin Harrison were interested in acquiring naval bases or even annexing it, but other elements of the government were not. Theodore Roosevelt enunciated his famous Corollary to the Monroe Doctrine because of the Dominican Republic's chaotic financial involvements with Europe and stretched his constitutional prerogatives by taking over its customhouses in 1905. Woodrow Wilson further stretched them in 1916 by occupying the country and setting up a lackluster naval administration to govern it. Only minor benefits were experienced while the rich and advanced United States ruled. Dramatic transformation of underdeveloped lands was not in vogue until later years. Despite some criticism of the arrogant nature of the American occupation, public opinion in the United States was indifferent.[1]

Table 2

The Reds	The Blues
1. Called the Party of Baez and the Regeneration	1. Known by the names of Liberal and National Party
2. Principal followers were farmers and poor town dwellers, persons seeking military opportunity	2. Principal followers were intellectuals and young people with hope of progress
3. Majority-based* and more ethnically Dominican, more realistic	3. Minority-based* and more idealistic
4. More conservative and pro-annexation	4. More liberal and nationalistic
5. Sought power by any means necessary	5. Defended the ideas of the Constitution, peace, and human rights
6. Leader was Báez; their intellectual leader was Félix María Delmonte	6. Leaders were Gregorio Luperón, Pedro Francisco Bonó, Arturo de Meriño, Ulises Francisco Espaillat, and others
7. Joined by a small group of followers of deceased leader Pedro Santana	7. Joined by a larger group of followers of deceased leader Pedro Santana.

Source: Peguero and de los Santos, Visión General, 225.
*These attributes can be misleading because Báez alienated people through his repressive policies, thus greatly increasing the popularity of the Blues in any term of his presidency. Also, most of Báez's followers probably had no idea of the concept of annexation to the United States.

In the Dominican Republic itself, politics were essentially reduced to a fratricidal struggle between the "Reds" and the "Blues." The Blues were based mostly in the Cibao and the Reds could be found in the south and southwest regions of the country. The economy and ecology of each region largely determined the resulting political stances. In the Cibao, the activity of tobacco-growing and related industries, which employed both men and women fairly regularly, created a more liberal population. Consequently the Blues paid lip service to the ideals of Duarte. In the south and west, woodcutting and lumbering were the major economic activities. Cyclical, sporadic, and subject to layoffs, this type of work produced an idle, listless population more disposed to following conservative *caudillos,* such as Báez.[2] Table 2 lists the chief attributes of the two factions.

In any event, the Dominican people as a whole were removed from any governmental processes except as soldiers in numerous revolutionary movements.[3] So removed from the entire annexation struggle were the people of both the United States and the Dominican Republic that in the end it came down to key actions by both proannexationists and antiannexationists that turned the tide against annexation of the Dominican Republic to the United States. This fact reflects the indifference of the U.S. public, who simply had no conception of the existence of the Dominican Republic. It also reflected the near-total ignorance of the Dominican people, who followed their *caudillos* dutifully.

The reality of this post-*Restauración* period was very different from the newspaper reports of the time, which actually measured only the strength of the antagonists in the annexation fight.[4] Both sides had access to newspaper editors. Mrs. Cazneau could easily express her views in the *New York Herald*[5] and the Haitian minister to Washington, M. Stephen Preston, was said to have had $20,000 at his disposal to influence the press, according to Hamilton Fish.[6]

In addition to making a pact with Báez to consummate the annexation of the Dominican Republic to the United States, Cazneau and Fabens were preparing for the riches that would surely come if annexation became a reality. In 1868 they set out to secure from Báez's Dominican government as many concessions as they could so that substantial financial rewards would come their way once U.S. capital and people started arriving. Fabens secured a lucrative concession for mineral exploration.[7] To finance it Cazneau and Fabens launched the Santo Domingo Company, with notable U.S. financiers as backers.[8] In addition, Cazneau secured claims to copper mines at various Dominican locations, while Fabens obtained a perpetual grant from the U.S. Senate giving him 1,683 feet of land fronting the most valuable part of Samaná Bay.[9] With these arrangements in place, one can easily imagine the satisfaction of Cazneau and Fabens when President Johnson read his annexation message to the U.S. Congress.

Their happiness was probably also fueled by a realistic appraisal of the nature of Báez's rule in the Dominican Republic and the resulting opportunities. According to historian Ricardo Pattee, this Báez presidency was one of the worst administrations in Dominican history.[10] So corrupt and repressive was this rule that historians speak of it as "the six years."[11] Ardent protectionist that he was, Báez preferred to focus his energies to that end. After having scared Seward into paying closer attention to the Dominican Republic, Báez had set about giving North Americans something they could negotiate over.

So it was that, before President Johnson's message to Congress, Seward had been met by Eugene Smith (son of U.S. commercial agent to the Dominican Republic J. Somers Smith), who was sent to Washington in November 1868 by Báez to lobby for annexation.[12] These negotiations had so turned Seward's head that, convinced of the efficacy of annexation, he had easily persuaded Johnson to give his congressional annexation speech of 9 December 1868. During these negotiations, which also had included J. Somers Smith, there arose a point that was to have important consequences in the annexation struggle. Before the younger Smith had arrived in Washington, Seward had sent a letter to his father saying that annexation should be supported by a popular plebiscite in the Dominican Republic, because otherwise it would violate the war powers of Congress and be tantamount to an act of war.[13] Although this point did not stop Johnson from endorsing annexation of not only the Dominican Republic but the entire island of Hispaniola, it forced Báez to go through the motions of holding a popular plebiscite at a later time, with disastrous consequences.

A day after Johnson's message to Congress, J. Somers Smith wrote Seward that Báez had written letters to different authorities in the Dominican Republic on the question of seeking U.S. protection and had received favorable replies. As a result of this display of unity in the Dominican Republic (which Báez implied was freely expressed), Báez, according to Smith, wanted immediate acceptance of the younger Smith's proposals and three U.S. war vessels dispatched to the island.[14] If Seward ever noticed the contradiction inherent in that message (the vessels would be used to fight Dominicans), he never broached the subject. Báez was to repeat such contradictions many times in the future, even in the face of opposing evidence. Soon, on 19 December 1868, J. Somers Smith, having received Seward's admonition concerning the war powers of Congress and the need to hold a plebiscite, wrote Seward that Báez was indeed anxious to demonstrate that the majority of Dominicans supported annexation. However, before this plebiscite could be held, Smith wrote, it would be advisable for the U.S. government to send a vessel of war and three hundred thousand dollars. If this happened, the U.S. government could take possession of Samaná and, in a little while, the Dominican people would apply for annexation. On the other hand, if the United States was not in favor of annexation, Báez would prefer that it purchase Samaná on the same terms that had been offered by Frederick Seward, the secretary's son, in January 1867.[15]

It is interesting to note that when this particular treaty had appeared before the Dominican Congress during José María Cabral's presidency, it was rejected because the Dominican constitution expressly forbade any foreign territorial sovereignty over Dominican soil. Báez quickly brushed aside any such considerations in his 1868–74 presidency.[16] The Báez government was even willing to forego the ratification process inherent in a treaty such as the one offered by Frederick Seward. Felix Delmonte, Dominican minister of justice and public instruction, appeared before J. Somers Smith on 22 December 1868 to ask his opinion of the plan to have different Dominican provinces hoist the U.S. flag and proclaim by acclaimation that they were placing themselves under the United States government. According to Delmonte, this pro-U.S. feeling was so strong that Báez would not be able to stop his fellow citizens, even if he were inclined to do so.[17] When that failed to evoke a favorable response, Báez decided to appeal to the fears of some U.S. officials and sent Delmonte to Smith with the message that Dominicans felt that merging with the United States would silence any European opposition.[18]

By January 1869 copies of Johnson's message to Congress had reached the Dominican Republic;[19] Báez, now more sure than ever that he had found at last the protector that he had been looking for for more than twenty-five years, quickly wrote approvingly to Johnson, saying that the majority of the people of the Dominican Republic were in favor of annexation.[20] Louis P. Augenard, a U.S. citizen, was selected to go to Washington and arrange for annexation by explaining to Seward the "real" situation in the Dominican Republic.[21] Fabens, who had expressed his desire to be of further assistance, was instructed by Manuel Gautier, Dominican minister of foreign relations, to go to Washington as well and present to Seward an official instruction relating to extending U.S. protection over the Dominican Republic.[22] At this time Fabens was in New York City, and he was to spend a good part of January 1869 trying to recruit influential congressmen to his position. One of his converts was Benjamin F. Butler, who already could see personal financial rewards for his support.[23] In fact, Butler was privy to the workings of Fabens's Samaná Bay Company, which, as has been noted, included valuable frontage on Samaná Bay. Butler advised Fabens to arrange for a lease or purchase soon, before the American ship that Báez had requested arrived.[24]

Fabens also attended to his Dominican responsibilities diligently and on 11 January 1869 wrote to both Seward and Butler that he had been instructed to tell them that the Dominican Republic wanted U.S. protection.[25] This was very important because for any resolution providing for the extension of North American protection over the Dominican Republic to be introduced in the U.S. House of Representatives, it was necessary to have concrete evidence that the Dominicans wanted such action.[26] The next step was taken on 12 January 1869, when Gen. Nathaniel P. Banks, chairman of the House Committee on Foreign Affairs, sponsored a resolution that authorized the president to extend U.S. protection to the governments of Haiti and the Dominican Republic. Banks based his resolution on the fact that the two republics of Hispaniola apparently wanted this protection. He also said that unless the two republics voluntarily agreed to this, no further action would follow. This is a protection from revolution, Banks stated, not protection in the European sense.[27] Because most members of the House feared that this resolution would result in entanglement in the domestic problems of unstable governments, the resolution was tabled by a vote of 126 to 36.[28]

However, help was on the way. By this time Augenard had arrived and quickly set out to resurrect the annexation scheme.[29] It was pointed out by Seward that the House vote did not necessarily indicate a permanent setback. When Banks asked Seward about the situation in the Dominican Republic, Seward told Banks on 29 January 1869 that Augenard was arriving with a "reliable and confidential proposition [coming] from the Dominican Republic which proposes immediate annexation, waives all preliminary stipulations, and addresses itself simply to the discretion and friendship of the United States . . . [and the matter was] entirely confidential."[30] Banks now had a problem of the first order. When he had introduced his 12 January resolution, he had stated explicitly that U.S. protection would not lead to annexation. Now, confronted with information that the Dominican government wanted annexation, Banks's earlier resolution seemed either misleading and/or misguided. He therefore could not shame himself by calling for annexation.[31]

Other congressmen were willing to do so, however. On 1 February 1869 Representative Orth of Indiana introduced a resolution calling for annexation of the territory of "San Domingo" with the following conditions: (a) that the people of the Dominican Republic adopt a republican form of government; (b) that this action be taken with the people's consent; (c) that this action be submitted for U.S. Congressional approval; and (d) that this action should ultimately lead to the establishment of a state government of republican form.[32] Although by now many newspapers evidently favored the resolution[33] and—incredibly—Seward was of the opinion that even Haiti desired this action,[34] the measure was defeated 110–63.[35] That this vote was much closer than the Banks resolution was not lost on annexation proponents, who were by now in different parts of the United States.[36] Desiring to reassure Báez that all was not lost, Seward wrote to J. Somers Smith on 5 February 1869 to explain the reason for the adverse vote. According to him, Congress was hesitant because it did not have the confidential, proannexation information that the State Department possessed and that present domestic problems were causing difficulty. Seward hastened to add that the thrust of annexation was in harmony with the general sentiments of the people and government of the United States.[37] To rectify this legislative ignorance, Seward than wrote Nathaniel P. Banks that "important despatches touching a subject that has been before the House of Representatives, have this day been received from the City of St. Domingo. These despatches Mr. Seward would like to show to General Banks or to any other member of the Committee of Foreign Relations who may do him the honor to call here in the course of tomorrow."[38]

Since one of the matters bothering Banks and others was the Dominican debt, Seward decided to address that matter also. He saw Representatives Orth and Cullom the next day to assure them that the Dominican debt was "nominal" and not more than half a million dollars. Asked for evidence to support that contention, Seward told these gentlemen that they would have to take him "on faith."[39] Meanwhile, Banks was slowly being converted into a proponent of annexation. First, Seward was able to provide him "evidence" of the low Dominican debt,[40] and second, Banks was soon to come under the influence of Colonel Fabens, who wrote to Banks on 18 February 1869 to thank him for favorable correspondence that would enable him to communicate to the Dominican people the receptiveness of the U.S. to annexation.[41] To prepare Báez for what was coming, Seward had written J. Somers Smith on 15 February 1869 that Banks wanted precise information on conditions in the Dominican Republic. To this end Fabens was to proceed to the Dominican Republic for "fact-finding."[42]

It was now evident that, notwithstanding the earlier negative House votes on the Dominican Republic, the subject of Dominican annexation would be sure to reappear in the U.S. Congress. The proannexationists were now content to bide their time until the advent of the administration of U.S. Civil War hero Ulysses S. Grant.[43]

The arrival of Grant had far-reaching implications in the annexation fight. Although Johnson favored annexation, this issue was clearly not of paramount concern to him. Moreover, in spite of his recent impeachment, Johnson's administration did not go down in history as

Hamilton Fish. *(Courtesy of the Library of Congress.)*

the most corrupt one in the U.S. presidency. Grant, however, was a man who was susceptible to the ideas of Cazneau, Fabens, and Báez. Not only was Grant obsessed with the idea of Dominican annexation, which he considered equal to colonial expansion,[44] but he had the type of personality and tastes that attracted "confidence men."[45] Like most generals, he had a tenacity of purpose and a keen knowledge of the resources at his disposal.[46] Although Dominican annexation was never a real desire of the North American people, lawmakers, or public opinion arbiters,[47] Grant, aware that nearly all these factions did want harmony within the Republican party, made the support of Dominican annexation a prerequisite for party unity.[48] He also utilized to the limit the services of his secretary of state, Hamilton Fish, who possessed great loyalty to his chief and good diplomatic skills.[49]

Because twentieth-century Dominicans and Haitians regard Senator Charles Sumner, the leader in the legislative fight against annexation, as a hero,[50] they tend to think that only Sumner was responsible for the ultimate failure of the plan to make the Dominican Republic a part of the United States.[51] However, Sumner's role has been overemphasized. He indeed spearheaded the antiannexation fight, which he regarded as a crusade to preserve the rights of colored people.[52] Moreover, as the battle wore on, Sumner, never known for his ability to compromise his opinions,[53] came to detest the aims and tactics of the supporters of annexation.[54] But there were other eloquent voices against annexation as well, such as that of Senator Carl Schurz.[55] In addition, Sumner never needed much help in generating opposition to the idea of annexation because it was never that popular in the first place. If the Republicans went along with Grant on annexation, it was probably because they dreaded less the prospect of annexation than the idea of dividing the Republican party from its chief.[56] W. Stull Holt has posited that most votes against annexation were probably not due to Sumner's influence, but, on the other hand, votes for annexation were probably due to Grant's pressuring tactics.[57] Indeed, as the annexation battle continued, Grant designated for punishment not only recalcitrant senators like Sumner, but took action against anyone in his cabinet opposed to annexation.[58]

For his part, Fish had another reason for supporting Grant in the fight for annexation. It happened that both Grant and Sumner favored using a hostile tone toward Great Britain in connection with the "Alabama Claims," which were for Fish a diplomatic problem of the first order. As Current and his coauthors explain:

The United States had a burning grievance against Great Britain which had originated during the Civil War. At that time the British government, according to the American interpretation, had violated the laws of neutrality by permitting the Confederate cruisers, the *Alabama* and others, to be built and armed in the English shipyards and let loose to prey on Northern commerce. American demands that England pay for the damages committed by these vessels became known as the "Alabama Claims." Although the British government realized its diplomatic error in condoning construction of the cruisers (in a future war American-built *Alabamas* might operate against Britain), it at first hesitated to submit the issue to arbitration. Seward tried earnestly to settle the Alabama claims before leaving office. Secretary Fish continued to work for a solution, and finally in 1871 the two countries agreed to the Treaty of Washington, one of the great landmarks in international pacification.[59]

By diverting the attention of these two formidable individuals to the annexation of a small, relatively meaningless island nation, Fish could pursue his diplomacy and at the same time reduce the habitual interference of Sumner.[60]

A noticeable rift between annexation factions of North Americans in the Dominican Republic became noticeable during the change of administration. By this time J. Somers Smith was leery enough of the activities of Fabens to have requested an audience with Báez to talk about it. Báez cleverly diverted some of Smith's concerns, and the result was a 9 March 1869 memo from Smith to Seward that acknowledged the receipt of Seward's 15 February letter requesting information on the Dominican Republic. The memo also contained a description of Báez's "true" opinion of Fabens. According to Smith, Báez was suspicious of Fabens's character and diplomatic status. Furthermore, Fabens was not an accredited agent of the Dominican Republic and had only been asked to find out the doings of the (previous) Cabral administration and the actual proposals made by the Dominican government for the purchase of Samaná.[61] At that very moment, however, Fabens was presenting to Hamilton Fish and Ulysses Grant a memorandum stating that the Dominican Republic was now disposed to enter the Union as a new state, like Texas.[62]

Although little explanation would have been needed to provide a reason for such a misrepresentation on the part of Báez, some revolutionary activity on the part of the ousted president, General Cabral, and his ally, General Gregorio Luperón, was influential as well. In addition to harassing Báez's government, these leaders had been using Haitian territory for mounting their attacks.[63] Their associates in Haiti were opponents of Haitian President Salnave, who happened to be an ally of Báez.[64] On 11 March 1869, Cabral, Luperón, and General Pablo Pujol, along with aid from Haitian revolutionary leader Nissage Saget, entered into an agreement of joint Haitian–Blue party support.[65] This agreement, which also involved tactical military strategy, sent Cabral south and Luperón north to eventually start naval-based operations.[66]

One can surmise that Seward breathed a sigh of relief that soon he would no longer be forced to deal with so much contradictory information. It would be left up to Fish to decipher what was true and what was not. On one of Seward's last days as secretary of state he received a note from J. Somers Smith, sent on 19 March 1869 and accompanied by a report prepared by Delmonte on conditions in the Dominican Republic.[67] If sending this separate report meant that Smith was expressing his disapproval of Fabens and his refusal to work with him, it did not deter Fabens from sending a telegram to Nathaniel P. Banks on 24 March 1869 stating that matters were now "fully arranged."[68] When Smith later confronted Báez once again with a demand to spell out the status of Fabens, he again received evasive replies.[69]

Fabens, now in the United States, had managed to see Grant, and when he presented his 9 March proposal he had little difficulty in convincing Grant of the advantages of Dominican annexation.[70] Soon Fabens was asked by Banks to draft a report for the benefit of the members of the House Committee on Foreign Affairs concerning the financial and political conditions of the Dominican Republic.[71] Fabens, who had prepared a false report months in advance, made the trip to preserve the illusion of objectivity, stayed in the Dominican Republic for thirty-six hours, and returned to Washington, where he gave Banks a memorandum stating that the total indebtedness of the Dominican Republic was not more than $600,000 and that the Dominican people fervently wanted annexation to the United States.[72] On 1 April 1869 Fabens wrote to Hamilton Fish, now secretary of state, enthusiastically describing the Dominican situation.[73] Later a similar but more subdued communication came from J. Somers Smith.[74]

To help ease any apprehensions preoccupying the Dominican people on annexation, Báez had been telling various stories, eventually saying that the United States was really a collection of free and independent republics, each state or republic containing its own religion, language, habits, and customs. Later, when even this failed to convince some doubters, he would resort to brutal repression.[75] The workings of government cost money, however, and Báez was desperately in need of it. According to Sumner Welles, by the spring of 1869 Báez's government had serious financial difficulties,[76] and so Fabens, on 21 April 1869, wrote to Fish that Samaná Bay could be leased from the Dominican government at an annual rate of

$100,000.[77] However, Báez needed money immediately and could not wait for the U.S. government to respond. He soon turned to other sources.

On 8 May 1869 a man named Edward H. Hartmont (formerly Edmond Hertzberg[78]) visited the Dominican Republic from London and got a concession to remove and sell guano from the island of Alta Vela.[79] He soon returned to London with a commission to serve as the consul-general of the Dominican Republic, together with a contract dated 1 May 1869 that called for a loan of £420,000. Hartmont was to receive £100,000; he also was to pay the Dominican government £320,000 by 31 December 1869. The sum of £50,000 was paid to the Dominican government (Báez claimed he only got £38,000) on the day the contract was signed. The Dominican government was to pay £58,900 annually for twenty-five years, making the total payback on this loan, which was for an interest rate of 18 percent per annum, £1,472,000.[80] That these terms were almost tantamount to loansharking is self-evident; however, they can also be considered an indication of the desperation of the Báez government, which was encountering more and more opposition at home.[81] In addition, the enormous debt engendered by this loan indirectly led to later financial blunders by Báez's presidential successors, resulting in increased susceptibility to U.S. "Dollar Diplomacy" in the twentieth century.[82]

In May 1869, J. Somers Smith, the U.S. commercial agent, who by now was one of the few North Americans in the Dominican Republic disposed to send any discouraging information back to the United States, informed Fish that Báez had entered into the Hartmont loan for £420,000, which was to be guaranteed by a portion of the customs receipts in Santo Domingo City and Puerto Plata. In addition, said Smith, there were other concessions given to Hartmont, the details of which had not been publicized.[83] Smith then once again cornered Báez and this time asked him if he had considered the consequences of the loan for annexation. Báez answered that the Dominican government had only received a small amount of the loan and that it was only a temporary measure.[84] Smith then informed Fish on 18 May 1869 that the Dominican government was still strongly in favor of annexation as the only means of saving their nation from ruin.[85]

It was now evident to the advocates of annexation that the next step was to bring the subject of Dominican annexation before the Congress of the United States. To this end, a way had to be found to broaden the base of support for annexation. On 22 May 1869 the investment house of Spofford, Tileston and Company (of which Fabens was an agent) invited Banks and other members of the House

Committee on Foreign Affairs for a Dominican junket. According to Tansill:

> They [the committee] would see, of course, only what Fabens and his clique would arrange for them to see, and there was always the possibility that some members of the committee might find it to their material advantage to espouse the cause of annexation.[86]

Although Banks and the others declined, it was not due to any actions of the part of Fabens, who had instructed the investment house to delay for several days the departure of their steamer.[87] Meanwhile, back in the Dominican Republic, opposition was continuing. On 1 June 1869 Luperón gave a spirited patriotic speech in Puerto Plata in which he pointed out the dangers of annexation. He continued his naval activities shortly afterwards, in which, by the use of his small steamer, the *Telégrafo,* he was able to transport revolutionary troops across the north coast of the Dominican Republic.[88] Eventually the *Telégrafo* caused so much trouble that Luperón, who had gained fame as a fighter in the *Restauración* against Spain, was declared a pirate by the Dominican government on 19 June 1869.[89] Although Luperón had to sell the *Telégrafo* at the end of 1869, it was to greatly occupy the attention of the Dominican government until then.[90]

Faced with the seeming contradictions of the correspondences of Fabens and Smith, as well as the duplicities of Báez, Fish decided to send a special agent down to the Dominican Republic to give a true report of conditions there. On 2 June 1869 Fish sent instructions to Benjamin Hunt of Philadelphia to go to the Dominican Republic and give a detailed report on the character of its population, the natural resources, the commerce, and the extent of its public debt. Hunt was also to ascertain the true disposition of the Dominican people toward annexation to the United States.[91] When Hunt, for health reasons, declined this assignment, Colonel Fabens offered his services and promptly caught the same Spofford, Tileston and Company steamer that had been waiting to take the members of the House Committee on Foreign Affairs on their Dominican "fact-finding" cruise.[92] In addition to transporting Fabens for this special mission, this particular trip served other purposes as well. Spofford, Tileston and Company soon was able to establish a concession for a steamship line from Santo Domingo City to New York.[93]

Fabens also had matters to discuss with Báez, for Báez clearly was getting impatient with the lack of response by the U.S. government to his annexation efforts.[94] For Báez, whose experience in and respect for democratic institutions was minimal, the fact that even with the enthusiastic support of Grant (whose eagerness for annexation was conveyed to Báez by Fabens) the United States had still not annexed the Dominican Republic must have seemed difficult to fathom. He was now more than ever willing to say or do anything necessary to get into the fold of the United States and to avoid the retribution señors Luperón and Cabral surely had in store for him. Thus it was that when J. Somers Smith called on him and told him that, in his opinion, the annexation matter had been delayed because of activities of such men as Augenard and Fabens, Báez replied that neither individual had been authorized to carry on activities or negotiations that would result in annexation.[95] In any event, the Dominican president's financial woes continued; he soon instructed Smith to inform Fish that he believed it was necessary to have confidential negotiations and if the United States could give him assurances of cooperation and two war vessels, along with $200,000, it could take possession of Samaná Bay and the arrangements for annexation could immediately begin.[96]

One reason for the duplicity of Báez and other Dominican officials concerning the status of Fabens was, in addition to the financial crisis of the Dominican government, the knowledge that the United States had previously ignored a Dominican request for assistance through normal channels.[97] Therefore they were quite willing to use any and all agents at their disposal. On 22 June 1869 Dominican officials secretly urged Fabens to return at once to the United States and push forward plans for annexation. Manuel Gautier explicitly asked Fabens to seek a "method of conferring with President Grant and his influential friends there and explain these views."[98] The whole affair had taken a more serious turn. Fabens was now committed to bringing President Grant in as a force behind annexation.

Plotting his strategy carefully, Fabens, upon arriving in the United States, first wrote Senator Charles Sumner, chairman of the Senate Committee on Foreign Relations, on 1 July 1869, trying to win Sumner over to the idea of annexation as a means of saving the Dominican Republic much "bloodshed" and "anarchy."[99] He then completed his responsibility to Secretary Fish, who had asked Benjamin Hunt make a report on the Dominican Republic that Fabens had undertaken in Hunt's absence. On 9 July 1869 Fabens wrote Fish of the ardent desire of the Dominican Republic for annexation to the United States. Further, he requested that some "suitable person" be immediately sent to the Dominican Republic to study the situation there and to make a "true and accurate report of the present political situation of that island."[100] If Fish hesitated to carry out that request, his reluctance was overcome by President Grant. As Welles writes,

> Persuaded of the advantages of the annexation project as explained to him by Fabens, attracted by the glory which he imagined would ensue to his Administration by adding to the domains of the United States, and convinced by the favorable reception given the propaganda from the pen of Mrs. Cazneau and other interested persons which such influential papers as the *New York Herald* were publishing with increased frequency that public opinion was in accord with the opinions which he himself had formed, President Grant definitely committed himself to the annexation program.[101]

Not only was this "suitable person" quickly selected, but, through the insistence of Grant, he turned out to be General Orville E. Babcock. Babcock was a member of an influential group of men surrounding the president. A former military secretary to Grant, he was often in a position to make his advice and persuasion felt. In addition, Babcock had married a girl from Grant's hometown and thoroughly recognized the value of friendly ties to the intensely loyal president. A pragmatist, Babcock was not adverse to the potential financial rewards of the annexation project and, in him, Fabens found a true ally.[102]

On 13 July 1869, Fish instructed Babcock to find out as much as possible about the Dominican government and people, especially

Union General Ulysses S. Grant and his staff at City Point, Virginia, 1864. Orville Babcock is in the extreme right. *(Courtesy of Perkins Library, Duke University.)*

with regard to their feelings about the United States and annexation. He also took care to direct Babcock to ascertain national revenues and the stability of the Dominican government.[103] To further impress President Báez, Babcock was also given a letter of credence from Grant in which Babcock was described in glowing terms.

During this time, Grant made another decision with far-reaching consequences: he would provide direct military aid to the Báez government. On 10 July 1869 Commander E. K. Owen was instructed to immediately sail to Dominican waters and start a search for Luperón's *Telégrafo*.[104] Three days later Owen was given additional orders to remain at Samaná or on the Dominican coast while Babcock was in the Dominican Republic and "give him the moral support of your guns."[105] Although scholars have surmised that Babcock, a military man, was chosen because of the revolutionary activities of Luperón and Cabral, his subsequent collusions with Cazneau and Fabens leave little doubt as to the more likely motivations for his selection. On 17 July 1869 Babcock left New York for the Dominican Republic on the steamer *Tybee,* which was owned by Spofford, Tileston and Company. Present were Fabens and other proannexation individuals such as Senator Cornelius Cole and "Judge" Peter J. O'Sullivan.[106] When they arrived in the Dominican Republic, Babcock, who knew little French and even less Spanish, was advised by Báez that Cazneau would be his interpreter.[107] Babcock took care to relate to Báez that as a military officer he had limited powers and had no authority whatsoever to make a treaty. At best he only could draw an outline of a treaty that, if it met with the approval of Fish and Grant, later could be formally negotiated and signed.[108]

Babcock stayed in the Dominican Republic for several weeks, conferring with Dominican officials and signing, together with Gautier on 4 September 1869, an outline that provided for a treaty of annexation. The acceptance of this treaty would obligate the United States to liquidate the public debt of the Dominican Republic. Included in this outline were three articles: article 1 bound Grant to use all his influence on Congress and to make no communication to that body until he could be sure of the success of annexation. Article 2 provided for the eventuality that the U.S. government could be hostile to annexation. Should this happen, the United States would buy Samaná for two million dollars. Article 3 provided that the United States would pay the Dominican government $150,000 for "defraying the unavoidable expenses of state" in the form of $100,000 in cash and $50,000 in arms.[109]

Inasmuch as Grant was now firmly behind annexation, it was soon apparent that the U.S. commercial agent, J. Somers Smith, would have to be replaced. Even before Gautier had written Fish to compliment Babcock, Smith had expressed to Fish grave doubts about the whole affair. According to Smith, Babcock had only consorted with Cazneau and Fabens, whom Smith now regarded as selfish speculators.[110] Smith's admonitions had little effect on Grant's commitment to annexation, however. On Babcock's return to the United States, Grant held an extraordinary cabinet meeting in which he announced that his aide had come back from the Dominican Republic with an informal treaty that could easily be changed into a formal one by having the U.S. consular agent sign it when they sent it back.[111] The irregularity of this proposed action, as well as the seeming disregard of the U.S. constitutional process, caught most cabinet members by surprise.[112] Fish especially was in an awkward position. Having been an intimate friend of Senator Charles Sumner, Fish had sought to keep him up to date on the Dominican annexation news: up to then he had told Sumner that Dominican annexation was gossip. Now his integrity and that of the State Department was in question: Fish felt compelled to offer Grant his resignation.[113] Grant quickly talked him out of resigning and Fish went on to become the only member of Grant's original cabinet to serve throughout his administration.[114]

Perhaps Grant's boldness could be traced to his military background or his crude instincts. On the other hand, it could have been that Grant was expecting a popular groundswell in favor of annexation, much like the expansionist fervor present at other times in U.S. history. At this juncture, James Gordon Bennett, editor and owner of the *New York Herald* and a person very strongly in favor of annexation, had decided to further the project by sending one of his reporters, DeBenneville R. Keim, to the Dominican Republic to discuss matters with Báez. Keim was instructed to send to Bennett proannexation materials and letters. The letters, to be published in the *New York Herald,* were expected to create a public sentiment friendly to U.S. expansion in the Caribbean.[115]

Thus it was that even before Babcock arrived in the Dominican Republic, Keim was already there, having arrived on 17 June 1869, and talking to Báez. Keim reported that Báez was a true patriot. For the benefit of North American racists, Keim informed his readers that Báez had an "off color" complexion with a "brunette face" and had a "very agreeable expression."[116] As a result of these remarks Báez gave Keim a letter for delivery to Grant in which the desire of the Dominican government for annexation was clearly expressed.[117]

Keim eventually delivered this letter while Grant was a guest at

Fish's estate in Garrison, New York. The message strengthened the president's resolve to push for annexation, and at this point he decided to send Babcock back for a second mission.[118]

While Keim and Báez had been engaging in mutual flattery, some notable Dominicans who had the misfortune to be at odds with Báez's annexation policy were quickly disappearing. Included in this group were poet and patriot Manuel Rodríguez Objío and *Restauración* hero Eusebio Manzueta.[119] Eventually, a growing colony of exiles fleeing the Báez government would make itself heard in letters of protest to the U.S. Congress.

To Grant's military mind, the task of accomplishing the annexation of the Dominican Republic must have seemed like an exercise in logistical planning. The cabinet had seemed disturbed that Babcock, a military officer not legally entitled to undertake negotiations with a foreign government, had seemingly entered into such arrangements. There were rumblings on the Hill that Senator Charles Sumner of Massachusetts would need to be reckoned with in order to push an annexation measure through the Senate. Finally, the presence in the Dominican Republic of a commercial agent who openly contradicted and undermined such persons as Cazneau and Fabens (who were indispensable to the annexation process, in Grant's view) was a nuisance at best and a danger at worst. The job of dealing with J. Somers Smith was the easiest. On 20 October 1869 Babcock sent a note to Fish saying that Grant thought that Major Raymond H. Perry should replace J. Somers Smith as the new U.S. commercial agent.[120]

The selection of Perry seems to have been made with the awareness of the company with which the new commercial agent would be soon associated. According to Tansill,

> Major Perry had achieved nothing worthy of commendation before being selected for his new post at Santo Domingo City. During his service in the Union Army he shot an officer who threatened his life, but was immediately acquitted by a court-marshal. Later, while on duty in New Orleans, he was implicated in the popular pastime of mule-stealing and sentenced to be dismissed from the army. Subsequently, he was restored to active duty and after the close of the Civil War was honorably discharged.[121]

Perry was also to sign the treaty that Babcock was expected to negotiate for annexation of the Dominican Republic. In addition Grant decided to send with Babcock General Delos B. Sackett, inspector-general of the U.S. army, ostensibly to act as an interpreter and to provide military counsel if needed.[122] On 3 November 1869, as Perry made his way on board the *Tybee*, which was to transport him to the Dominican Republic, he was met, "by chance," by Colonel Fabens, who proceeded to point the path that Perry was to follow in the upcoming negotiations. Adherence to this policy would be quite lucrative, according to Fabens.[123]

In Grant's mind, the cabinet would have to support him on annexation as well. The last component in Grant's plan (that of converting Sumner into an annexation proponent) would have to wait until Babcock returned with the treaty in hand.

On 18 November 1869 Babcock's party arrived in Santo Domingo City. Accompanying Sackett and Perry was also General Rufus Ingalls. Babcock had with him some detailed instructions from Fish dated 6 November 1869, and he also had draft treaties he was authorized to negotiate but that Major Perry was to sign, a ploy to keep up the pretense of Babcock not actually engaging in negotiations.[124] Babcock was to negotiate two treaties. One would annex the Dominican Republic to the United States as a territory. In order to eliminate the Dominican public debt the U.S. government was to promise $1.5 million to the Dominican government, which in turn was to promise that it would make no further grants or concessions and would contract no further debts until the United States took over. In order to take care of the immediate needs of the Dominican government, Babcock was authorized to advance one hundred thousand dollars as well as fifty thousand dollars worth of arms. The second treaty authorized a lease of Samaná Bay for ninety-nine years. During this leasing period the U.S. government would be obligated to pay the Dominican government an annual fee fixed by the negotiators. The government also would have the right to purchase Samaná Bay and its surroundings at any time for $2 million in gold.[125]

Included in Fish's instructions to Babcock was an admonition that Perry was not to sign any treaty with the Dominican government until the Hartmont loan was cancelled. However, Babcock was instructed to disregard the general instructions if Báez could not completely abrogate the Hartmont contract. In that case Babcock was to try to obtain the best terms possible. If it were not possible to "make arrangements" on the Hartmont contract, Grant would authorize Babcock to conclude a "convention and treaty in which the Dominican Republic shall assume all future obligations growing out of the contract."[126]

Fish also had ordered Perry to confer with Babcock and to be governed by his advice.[127] These instructions probably need not have been given, for when Perry had arrived in the Dominican Republic on 18 November 1869, he happened to encounter J. Somers Smith, the outgoing commercial agent, who took the time to give Perry a very

vivid picture of Dominican politics in general and the activities of
Cazneau and Fabens in particular. According to Smith, Cazneau was
the force behind this whole affair.[128] After Smith angrily left the
Dominican Republic, Cazneau quickly approached Perry and gave
him the same briefing as did Fabens. According to Cazneau,
Perry could get "a fine plantation and opportunities to handle money
for men in New York City" by cooperating.[129] Perry's caution in
responding to both Cazneau and Fabens was at first due to prudence.
In any event, since Perry had little direct influence, Cazneau opted to
concentrate on pushing through the treaty.

The people of Santo Domingo City soon became accustomed to the
scene that would repeat itself for days afterward. Each morning,
Babcock, Sackett, and Ingalls came ashore from a U.S. warship and
proceeded to the residence of Báez, where they negotiated. Sackett
acted as Babcock's interpreter, probably to Cazneau's chagrin. Báez
had as counsel his aides Gautier and Delmonte. Fabens and Cazneau
were invariably present.[130] Perry's role was minimal,[131] although he
later wrote a revealing letter to Fish that indicated the extent to which
the Dominican annexation scheme was one in which Cazneau,
Fabens, Babcock, and Ingalls all anticipated financial gain.[132] Of
course Báez also expected financial gain, but once again his un-
familiarity with the rules of procedure used in the United States
caused him to make the sorts of bribes that took Sackett and Babcock
by surprise. According to a congressional investigation, these negotiations had been delayed because the Dominican officials had wanted
to bribe Babcock—ostensibly for getting rid of Smith and having a
hand in harassing Luperón's Telégrafo. The real reason for the bribe,
which would give Babcock a grant in Samaná, was to secure support.
He hesitated because it would have violated article 6 of the treaty (that
no grants or concessions be made after the signing of the treaty). Báez
even wanted to tamper with the timing: he wanted to sign the treaty,
take it before his compliant Dominican Senate, give the land to
Babcock, and then put in article 6 two days later. Babcock never went
along because both he and Sackett were afraid it would militate
against the treaty in the United States.[133]

Perhaps the extent of time he spent in the tropics had blunted
General Cazneau's appreciation for the rules of parliamentary pro-
cedure as well, for as later revealed by Perry, Cazneau proposed
writing two separate drafts of the double treaties (one for the
Dominican Republic and one for the U.S. government). Although
Báez and Delmonte were enthusiastic about this plan, Babcock and
Perry both protested. Babcock felt it would put Grant in a bad
position and Perry thought it would deceive the Dominican people.

Báez and Delmonte then replied that this was only a fiction: they believed that if they did not succeed with annexation, it would cost them their lives.[134] Although Cazneau did not have the same fears, he had enough of a financial stake in the Dominican Republic to make other suggestions of his own. He urged that there should be a secret treaty if it looked as if there could be trouble with the "real" treaty. Sackett and Babcock said no to that as well.[135]

Báez knew that the Dominican Congress would be reluctant to lease Samaná or annex the Dominican Republic to the United States, even in the presence of his formidable powers of persuasion. To combat these problems he wanted to submit the treaty for the lease of Samaná to the Dominican Senate, calling it security for a loan advance (if annexation was put into effect, the question of a Samaná lease would be moot). This particular guise of the treaty could never go back to the United States because it would reveal to the U.S. government that instead of pushing through a lease for Samaná, Báez had simply arranged for a loan security.[136] In this manner Báez had hoped to deceive both the Dominican and U.S. lawmakers. Further, because he knew that most of the Dominican Congress would oppose annexation, he needed to alter the treaty for that reason also. He wanted to refer the question of the Dominican annexation to his people, whom he felt he could control. In a letter to Fish, Perry described the atmosphere present at the plebiscite Báez was to hold later on:

> . . . a list was opened in the police headquarters for citizens to register their names. Báez and Delmonte have told me several times that if any man opposed annexation they would either shoot him or send him his passports. They have also told me that it should be a free vote of the people but such has not been the case. There was much feeling throughout the Island kept in check and the people were not permitted to express any opposition to annexation. I have seen Báez myself shake his fist in the face of some of his nearest friends, amongst whom were officers of the army, in Báez' own house, and tell them he would banish them from the Island if they opposed annexation. This conduct on the part of Báez made many who were in favor of annexation opposed to it and also to him. . . . The prisons are filled with political prisoners.[137]

Babcock and Sackett refused to accede to Baez's suggestions for a secret treaty for Samaná[138]; however, the Dominican president was to have more success in "convincing" his fellow citizens to support annexation. He managed to quiet the fears of his fellow Dominicans and Gautier and Perry signed a treaty of annexation of the Dominican Republic to the United States on 29 November 1869. Since, as the annexation treaty was constructed, the lease of Samaná was to be a security pending the ratification of the annexation of the Dominican Republic by the United States,[139] Báez had had to procure authority from the Dominican Senate the previous day in order to sign the convention for the lease of Samaná Bay.[140]

When the Samaná treaty and the annexation treaty were both signed, Perry wrote to Fish, "in accordance with his instructions, General Babcock immediately turned over to Dominican officials approximately the sum of $150,000." On 4 December 1869 Generals Babcock, Sackett, and Ingalls went to Samaná Bay to raise the U.S. flag and take formal possession.[141]

An understanding of the exact status of the Samaná treaty as it related to the treaty of annexation is important. The lease of Samaná was to be a security for arms and cash advanced to the Dominican government, as Báez had indicated;[142] however, it was also linked to annexation in that the possession of Samaná was to remain in effect until the ratification of the treaty of annexation by the U.S. Senate.[143] As General Babcock later said, "this convention contained articles which referred to the subject of annexation; in other words, the two were constructed as to refer to the other."[144] Furthermore, in this case the possession of Samaná was not subject to ratification by the U.S. Congress.[145] This suited Fabens perfectly since he now controlled a valuable part of the Bay frontage with his Samaná Bay Company.[146]

The signing of the two treaties touched off a storm of protest from within and without the Dominican Republic. The Báez initiatives not only further alarmed Dominican opponents to Báez's repressive government, but also distressed those opposing annexation.[147] Soon a long protest signed by Generals Luperón and Cabral against the signing of the lease of Samaná Bay made its way to the United States.[148]

In the meantime Babcock had not been able to secure the abrogation of the Hartmont contract before the signing of the treaties for Samaná's lease and Dominican annexation. But, as discussed earlier, Grant had prepared for that eventuality. On 3 December 1869 Báez wrote Babcock that Hartmont was not capable of the loan balance due the Dominican government by 31 December 1869. Báez cleverly informed Babcock that if the Dominican government were to receive the Hartmont loan balance before that date, it would await instructions from Washington and "until we know whether, in the case of our refusing to receive it, the Government of the United States will take upon itself the consequences of such refusal."[149]

Here again someone had to save Báez from his own greed. He had already jeopardized the success of the annexation negotiations by trying to mislead in his reference to the status of Cazneau and Fabens;

he had also tried to bribe his way into the confidence of Babcock. In both cases he had come out relatively unscathed, in the latter case because of Babcock's knowledge of U.S. policy and in the former instance because Grant was already so committed to annexation that he would have listened to even General Robert E. Lee if his illustrious battlefield adversary had been an annexation proponent. Now, with the signed treaties now before him, Grant had to delicately confront this new problem. Tansill writes,

On December 21, President Grant called a meeting of his Cabinet, and the matter of the two treaties with the Dominican Republic came up for discussion. The President requested Secretary Fish read the treaty of annexation, and then he enjoined secrecy with reference to it until after January first. It was permissible, however, to refer to the treaty for the lease of Samaná Bay and to lead the public to suppose that it was the "only treaty." This procedure was advisable because the contract for the Hartmont loan would expire on December 31, and so far its terms had not been fulfilled by the banking house itself. The delay was due to the fact that this English banking house was of the opinion that it need not pay strict attention to the exact letter of the contract. In view of the desperate straits of the Dominican Government it was believed that even though the money due it by the Hartmont contract was not paid within the stipulated time, that government would still be glad to receive it and would waive any technical infraction of the contract. The news of the signature of a treaty for the lease of Samaná would not unduly disturb the directors of this banking house, but it was very possible that if they learned of a proposed treaty of annexation they would hasten to fulfill the terms of the contract and thus would secure valuable concessions that would seriously militate against the advisability of American annexation.[150]

For his part, Perry was now drawing conclusions of his own. Being more aware than anyone of his own reputation and military record, he now surmised that the annexationists had judged him as a man who would succumb to the offers of financial gain. Moreover, his recent conversations with his predecessor, J. Somers Smith, had convinced him that Smith had been the loser in a confrontation between Smith and the duo of Cazneau and Fabens.[151] On 28 December 1869 Perry sent Fish the following despatch:

I signed the treaty and followed the orders and advice of General Babcock as I was ordered to do, and am ready to carry out all orders that may be sent me, without personal or selfish motives which I regret to think influence some parties who have acted here in connection with this matter.[152]

What was going on in the mind of Secretary Fish? He knew fully that many of those connected with Dominican annexation were of questionable character. Since he knew Perry's background, to have received such a despatch from him must have left still more doubts in Fish's mind as to the level of these negotiations. However, one must remember that things were generally going according to plan for Fish. Although Senator Sumner had not yet entered center stage, Fish's superior, President Grant (one person who could harm the delicate negotiations necessary for the settlement of the Alabama Claims), was now eagerly pursuing half of an island. Under these circumstances Fish was willing to support the president and count on some respite from interference in his duties as secretary of state. However, he did have a confidant, and on 24 December 1869, having received an even earlier despatch from Perry alluding to dishonest behavior in the annexation negotiations, Fish wrote to Elihu Washburne, U.S. minister to France, giving him an outline of the two treaties. Although Fish enjoined Washburne to "observe the utmost confidence" about the two treaties,[153] it was hardly necessary since the New York press had given its readers an accurate view of what was to come.[154] North Americans interested in imperialism would have received a clear picture of President Grant's aims in the Caribbean just by reading a newspaper.[155]

Grant was now ready to attend to Senator Sumner. Coincidentally Sumner was also thinking about the Dominican Republic. He had received a disturbing letter from an associate suspicious of the activities of Cazneau and Fabens in the Dominican Republic,[156] and to address these concerns he decided to call on the president at the White House on 31 December 1869 for a conference regarding affairs in the Dominican Republic. Grant probably did not know that Sumner by this time had been receiving correspondence negatively describing Cazneau, Fabens, and Báez,[157] and so the president may have misunderstood Sumner's air of deep concern for the characteristic reserve of New Englanders. In any event, Sumner undoubtedly left that meeting with even more suspicions while Grant, characteristically naïve,[158] was convinced that he had a potential ally.

So convinced of this was the chief executive that he paid a call on the senator on the first Sunday of 1870. At that visit several misunderstandings were revealed and a few others were made. For example, Grant displayed an ignorance of Sumner's membership on the Senate Committee on Foreign Relations by constantly referring to him as being on the Senate Judiciary Committee.[159] Grant also seemed to be unaware that Sumner had expected him to ask for support for the request for expenditures Grant had made to cover Babcock's expenses in the Dominican Republic.[160] Grant did ask for Sumner's support for the treaty for Dominican annexation. In reply, Sumner said that he would support the president if he could, after he examined the information, a statement that caused the gravest of misunderstandings between the president and himself and that has been debated ever since.[161] However, the immediate outcome was that Grant left thinking that Sumner would support the treaty and Sumner believed that he had only promised to give the matter his consideration.[162] Much of the future bitterness between the two men (especially on the part of Grant) can be traced to this misunderstanding.[163]

Nevertheless, the start of New Year must have encouraged the president. He seemingly had garnered Senator Sumner's support for annexation and Babcock had returned with a signed treaty for both annexation and a lease of Samaná, which was now under U.S. control. The Hartmont banking house had not paid their loan balance to the Dominican government within the specified time. In addition, all looked well within the Dominican Republic:

> [All Dominicans were] well satisfied with the proposed change in sovereignty, and I believe that if a vote were to be taken today on the question of annexation, it would be decided in the affirmative without a dissenting voice. . . . On the Sunday following the raising of the U.S. flag, I attended service at the Wesleyan Chapel. . . . The chaplain, Revd. Jacob James, explained in a clear and forcible manner the character of the great political change about to take place. . . . The scene was very touching, for the whole congregation of several hundreds were responding with tears and sobs of grateful joy.[164]

That the author of the above description of joy was Colonel Fabens did not seem to concern Grant any more than had Sumner's evident air of concern over the Dominican annexation negotiations. In fact, if Grant had bothered to ask his military aide, he could have saved himself a lot of misunderstanding concerning Sumner, for shortly after the president's visit to Sumner's residence, Babcock had called on Sumner, and given him a copy of the treaty. Not only did Sumner become greatly disturbed when he saw Grant referred to as "His Excellency, General Ulysses S. Grant," but he strongly disapproved of the idea of Grant being a lobbyist to bring about the passage of a bill.[165] Good aide that he was, Babcock probably shielded his commander from this bad news, perhaps thinking that at some later date he or others could change Sumner's mind. Therefore, on 7 January 1870, thinking that he had Sumner's support, Grant signed vouchers from the Secret Service Funds authorizing payment to Babcock for incurred expenses and Spofford, Tileston and Company for rendering transportation.[166] Three days later he sent to the Senate the treaty for the lease of Samaná and the annexation of the Dominican Republic to the United States.[167]

The friendly *New York Herald* had foreseen this development,[168] but other newspapers were not as supportive as Grant had hoped.[169] Nevertheless the president sent out the call to exert all possible influence for passage of the treaty. From Major Perry came word that, according to Báez, the feeling in favor of the treaty was so great that even if Báez were disposed to do so, it would be impossible to stop it.[170]

In January 1870 Báez suffered a setback that changed the course of the annexation fight. Haitian President Salnave, who had supported Báez in spite of the fact that the Haitian people had an almost fanatical fear of the United States, was captured by General Cabral, who promptly turned him over to the Haitian revolutionary leader Nissage Saget. After a hasty trial, Salnave was placed before a firing squad and Nissage Saget became the Haitian president.[171] Now Báez was not only pressured by revolutionary leaders like Luperón and Cabral, but he could count on the opposition of the neighboring republic. The alarmed Báez government sent out a plea to Grant for military assistance.[172]

This event was a major turning point in the battle over annexation because it eventually brought into focus the legitimacy of the Báez government. If in fact Báez needed the assistance of the United States to continue as president, the question would naturally follow, "for what reason?" Moreover, if the Báez government was soliciting the help of an outside government to fight fellow Dominicans, additional doubts would be raised. Although Grant had previously authorized the U.S. navy to harass Luperón's *Telégrafo* during the previous summer and had sent Admiral Owen to support Babcock during the actual annexation negotiations, what was now called for was a sustained military presence.

Not seeing the implications, Grant conferred with the navy secretary and soon U.S. warships were sent to the Dominican Republic,[173] further convincing Senator Sumner that this treaty, which had previously been tarnished by the involvement of persons of dubious character, now implied serious constitutional breaches as well.[174] Sumner's previous doubts and misgivings soon converted into hardened opposition. The 7 February 1870 appearance of a petition hostile to annexation that made its way to the U.S. Senate from Dominican exiles living in Curaçao did little to lessen the opposition.[175]

Fabens, now in the United States, eventually tried to convert Sumner. Their subsequent conversation, which was reported in the

New York Tribune, only resulted in a wider gap between Sumner and advocates of annexation.[176] Grant's use of military force to assist Báez caused other problems as well that involved the actual legal basis for his intervention. Faced with the appearance that he had violated the war powers of Congress by sending warships to the Dominican Republic, Grant based his action on those taken by President Tyler when he signed the treaty calling for the annexation of Texas. At that time Tyler had promised that the United States would protect Texas from all foreign invasion while the treaty for annexation was pending in Congress.[177]

Grant was also able and willing to bend and turn the rules of diplomatic procedure to further the cause of annexation. Having failed to make an ally of Senator Sumner, Fabens next called upon the secretary of state for the same purpose, claiming to have been appointed an Envoy Extraordinary of the Dominican Republic for the purpose of expediting annexation to the United States. This was an unnecessary visit because Fish would have followed any directive emanating from Grant's office and Grant was already committed to annexation. However, during the visit Fabens made the blunder of stating that he had already seen the president before coming to Fish. Fish was greatly disturbed at that revelation because he knew it would lay the administration open to the charge that the treaty had been negotiated outside of regular channels. Apprised of Fish's displeasure, Grant took full responsibility for the behavior of Fabens and implied that the question of Dominican annexation was important enough to justify "any irregularities in the usual diplomatic procedure."[178]

Grant's Dominican counterpart was equally adept at circumventing procedure. Having promised his fellow citizens that there would be a plebiscite on annexation to the United States, Báez set out to make absolutely sure that this vote would be a rousing indication to all that the Dominican Republic desired annexation to the United States. So enthusiastic was the Dominican Republic to effect this expression of popular support for annexation that it went so far as to imprison a U.S. citizen, Mr. Davis Hatch, who it feared would somehow defeat the annexation treaties.[179] Báez also wanted U.S. warships present before the plebiscite was to be taken, and he wanted Senate ratification of the treaty before any final action was taken by the Dominican government. Major Perry, who had now developed sufficient insight into the frame of mind of J. Somers Smith some months before, decided to have a talk with Cazneau about this plebiscite. It seemed to Perry that such a plebiscite, replete with threats, improvised results, and imprisonments, would be difficult to undertake and that it should probably be delayed. Cazneau, completely misunderstanding the tenor of Perry's remarks, blurted that he held Báez between "his thumb and his finger" and that he would "compel him to have the vote at once."[180]

Partly as a result of Cazneau's efforts, an edict was announced on 16 February 1870, calling for a plebiscite on 19 February with reference to annexation to the United States.[181] On 20 February Perry was able to report that the vote was overwhelmingly favorable to annexation and that everything seemed "quiet and favorable."[182] This favorable situation was prefaced by a command from Báez to vote for annexation 16,000 to 11. The eleven votes against annexation were made to avoid suspicion.[183] Subsequently Gautier wrote two different letters to two different people, giving two different percentages of success.[184] Regardless of the manner in which this vote was obtained, however, the plebiscite was important because it satisfied article 4 of the treaty.

On the other hand, the imprisonment of Davis Hatch and the vague response by Dominican officials[185] had ramifications that far overshadowed the positive image given by the rigged plebiscite. It had the effect of setting into motion the processes that ultimately led to Raymond Perry's resignation as commercial agent. In fact, so disgusted was Perry with the whole affair that he has been credited with heroic behavior by at least one Dominican historian.[186]

As a result of Perry's agitation Hatch eventually was released in Perry's custody and sent to Havana.[187] By espousing the cause of Davis Hatch, Perry quickly fell out of step with the annexation clique. Both Cazneau and Gautier filed letters of disapproval to Perry over what they considered inappropriate behavior.[188] Perry would eventually write Fish a six-line resignation letter in July 1870.[189] More important, Hatch's imprisonment marked the second major setback for proponents of annexation because it resulted in much protest in the United States and the appointment of a U.S. Senate committee to investigate the matter. Although the majority report of this committee agreed with Cazneau and Fabens that Hatch was a "revolutionary," the minority report was favorable to Hatch and the necessity for an investigation weakened the stance of the proannexationists.[190] A Senate resolution passed on 21 February called for Fish to turn over all correspondence relating to Hatch's imprisonment.[191]

Suddenly the picture was a great deal darker for the proannexationists. The Senate debate over the treaty was to begin on 24 March 1870, and annexation opponents had more weapons at their disposal. It would now be much easier to oppose annexation legitimately without appearing to reject President Grant.

NOTES

1. Fagg, *Cuba, Haiti and the Dominican Republic*, 141. Reprinted by permission of the publisher, Prentice-Hall.

2. Peguero and de los Santos, *Visión General*, 224–25. Also see Frank Moya Pons, *Manuel de Historia Dominicana*, 7th ed. (Santiago: Universidad Católica Madre y Maestra, 1983), 404–5.

3. Monclús, *El Caudillismo*. See also Moya Pons, *Manuel de Historia*, 375, which documents the ignorance of the Dominican people concerning the facts of annexation.

4. For a listing of the best primary and secondary sources on the annexation struggle of 1869–71, see Charles C. Hauch, "Fuentes en los Estados Unidos Relativas al Proyecto de Anexión de la República Dominicana, 1869–1871," *Boletín del Archivo General de la Nación* 4 (August 1941): 183–87. Newspapers often participated directly in the annexation struggle. Tansill, *The United States and Santo Domingo*, 370, and Benjamin P. Hunt, "Newspaper History of the Annexation of the Dominican Republic from July 1869 to July 1870," 5 vols., Manuscript, Boston Public Library.

5. Welles, *Naboth's Vineyard*, 1:370.

6. Heinl and Heinl, *Written in Blood*, 255n; Logan, *Haiti and the Dominican Republic*, 46. Haitian propaganda may have influenced one of the leading opponents of annexation, Senator Charles Sumner of Massachusetts. See Montague, *Haiti and the United States*, 108.

7. Tansill, *The United States and Santo Domingo*, 344.

8. Ibid., 344–46.

9. U.S. Congress, Senate Executive Document No. 9, 42d Cong. 1st sess., 5 April 1871 (vol. 1, serial 1466), 30.

10. Ricardo Pattee, *La República Dominicana* (Madrid: Ediciones Cultura Hispana, 1967), 148.

11. Ian Bell, *The Dominican Republic* (Boulder, Colo.: Westview Press, 1981), 56. Báez has had his defenders. See Hazard, *Santo Domingo*, 271, and Schoenrich, *Santo Domingo*, 64–65. I have done what Schoenrich did: speculate on what would have happened had the Dominican Republic become a U.S. possession, but not necessarily with a decidedly pro-U.S. slant, as in his case.

12. J. Somers Smith to William H. Seward, 9 November 1868, vol. 5, 18 January 1864–19 December 1868, Despatches from United States Consuls in Santo Domingo 1837–1906, T 56/Roll 5.

13. Seward to Smith, 17 November 1868, vol. 12, 20 October 1868–17 November 1969, series 3, Instruction to Consuls, MS, Department of State, Washington, D.C.

14. Smith to Seward, 10 December 1868, vol. 5, Despatches, T 56/Roll 5.

15. Ibid., 19 December 1868.

16. Of the twenty constitutional changes made in the Dominican government over the years, Báez was responsible for five. See Monclús, *El Caudillismo*, and Osorio Lizarazo, *La Isla Iluminada*, 69.

17. Tansill, *The United States and Santo Domingo*, 271.

18. Smith to Seward, 9 January 1869, vol. 5, Despatches from U.S. Consuls, T 56/Roll 5.

19. Tansill, *The United States and Santo Domingo*, 272.

20. Buenaventura Báez to Andrew Johnson, 8 January 1869, vol. 2, 11 January

1869–17 July 1871, Notes from the Legations of the Dominican Republic in the United States to the Department of State 1844–1906, T 801/Roll 1.

21. Manuel Gautier to William H. Seward, ibid.

22. Joseph W. Fabens to Seward, 11 January 1869, ibid.

23. Tansill, *The United States and Santo Domingo*, 273.

24. Ibid., 274.

25. Joseph W. Fabens to William H. Seward, 11 January 1869, vol. 2, Notes from the Legations, T 801/Roll 1. See also Fabens to Benjamin F. Butler, 11 January 1869, Benjamin F. Butler Papers, Manuscript Division, Library of Congress, Washington, D.C.

26. Tansill, *The United States and Santo Domingo*, 274. Seward had previously received a similar expression of proannexation sentiment from the Dominican Republic. See Smith to Seward, 24 October 1868, vol. 5, Despatches from U.S. Consuls, T 56/Roll 5.

27. *Congressional Globe*, 40th Cong., 3d sess., 12 January 1869, 317–18. See also W. A. Dunning, "Paying for Alaska," *Political Science Quarterly* 27 (September 1912): 385–98.

28. *Congressional Globe*, 40th Cong., 3d sess., 13 January 1869, 340.

29. Louis P. Augenard to William H. Seward, 26 January 1869, vol. 2, Notes from the Legations, T 801/Roll 1.

30. William H. Seward to Nathaniel P. Banks, 29 January 1869, vols. 80–81, 14 December 1868–27 August 1869, Domestic Letters of the Department of State 1784–1906, National Archives and Records Service, GSA, Washington, D.C., M 40/Roll 65.

31. Tansill, *The United States and Santo Domingo*, 278.

32. *Congressional Globe*, 40th Cong., 3d sess., 1 February 1869, 769.

33. Tansill, *The United States and Santo Domingo*, 279.

34. Seward to President Andrew Johnson, 30 January 1869, vol. 10, 15 May 1868–15 January 1872, Reports of the Secretary of State to the President and Congress, MS, Department of State, Washington, D.C.

35. *Congressional Globe*, 40th Cong., 3d sess., 1 February 1869, 769.

36. Tansill, *The United States and Santo Domingo*, 280–81.

37. Seward to Smith, 5 February 1869, vol. 2, 30 December 1859–28 June 1871, Diplomatic Instructions of the Department of State 1801–1906, National Archives and Records Service, GSA, Washington, D.C., M 77/Roll 153.

38. Seward to Nathaniel P. Banks, 5 February 1869, vol. 10, 15 May 1868–15 January 1872, Reports.

39. Tansill, *The United States and Santo Domingo*, 282.

40. Seward to Banks, 6 February 1869, vol. 10.

41. Joseph W. Fabens to Banks, 18 February 1869, Nathaniel P. Banks Papers, Manuscripts Division, Library of Congress, Washington, D.C.

42. Seward to Smith, 15 February 1869, vol. 2, Diplomatic Instructions, M 77/Roll 153.

43. It is ironic that the annexation battle would turn into a bitter feud between two men who would achieve fame as champions of freedom: U. S. Grant, by virtue of his stint as victorious general in the Union army and Sumner for his abolitionist work. See Lerone Bennett, *Before the Mayflower* (Chicago: Johnson Publishing Co., 1962), 180.

44. Tansill, *The United States and Santo Domingo*, 338–39. In one of the most complete books written on Cuban history, *Cuba: The Pursuit of Freedom* (New York: Harper and Row, 1971), 246–51ff, Hugh Thomas discusses the U.S. role in the

Cuban 1868 rebellion. Desiring U.S. annexation, the rebels appealed to President Grant, who was then unwilling to directly sponsor annexation but wanted to grant the rebels belligerent status. He was talked out of this by Hamilton Fish, secretary of state. U.S. filibuster groups were also available for action.

45. Jacob D. Cox, "How Judge Hoar Ceased to be Attorney General," *Atlantic Monthly* 76 (August 1895): 173.

46. Avery Craven, *The United States: Experiment in Democracy* (Boston: Ginn and Co., 1962), 285.

47. Theodore C. Smith, "Expansion After the Civil War: 1865–1871," *Political Science Quarterly* 16 (September 1901): 428. See also Cox, "How Judge Hoar Ceased to be Attorney General," 165.

48. Tansill, *The United States and Santo Domingo*, 403–5.

49. Tansill (Ibid., 339) has observed that Fish was not the expansionist that Seward was, although Grant more than made up for this lack. See also Adam Badeau, *Grant in Peace* (Hartford, Conn.: S. S. Scranton & Co., 1887), 233. See also Allan Nevins, *Hamilton Fish* (New York: Dodd Mead and Co., 1936), chap. 1, 113, and Edward L. Pierce, *Memoirs and Letters of Charles Sumner*, 4 vols. (Boston: Roberts Brothers, 1877–93), 4:379.

50. Fagg, *Cuba, Haiti and the Dominican Republic*, 150. See also Jacinto Gimbernard, *Historia de Santo Domingo*, 7th ed. (Madrid: M. Fernández y Cia, S.A., 1978), 234–35, and Heinl and Heinl, *Written in Blood*, 255. According to Heinl and Heinl, Sumner's picture hangs in the Chamber in Port-au-Prince beside the Amis des Noirs of 1789.

51. Horace White, *Life of Lyman Trumbull* (New York: Houghton Mifflin Co., 1913), 342–43; John Sherman, *Recollections of Forty Years in the House, Senate and Cabinet*, 2 vols. (Chicago, New York: Werner Co., 1895), 1:470–73; Hugh McCulloch, *Men and Measures of Half a Century* (New York: Charles Scribners Sons, 1888), 234; James G. Blaine, *Twenty Years of Congress*, 2 vols. (Norwich, Conn.: Henry Bill Publishing Co., 1886), 1:458–63.

52. Logan, *Haiti and the Dominican Republic*, 44–45. See also McCulloch, *Men and Measures*, 234, who noted Sumner's abstract concern for people of color, coupled with his personal indifference to them.

53. McCulloch, *Men and Measures*.

54, Sherman, *Recollections*, 470–73.

55. See White, *Life of Lyman Trumbull*, 342–43, and Hans G. Trefousse, *Carl Schurz* (Knoxville: University of Tennessee Press, 1982), 186–95.

56. Frederic Bancroft and William Dunning, "A Sketch of Carl Schurz' Political Career," in *Reminiscences*, ed. Carl Schurz, 3 vols. (New York: The McClure Co., 1908), 3:325.

57. W. Stull Holt, *Treaties Defeated by the Senate* (Gloucester, Mass.: Peter B. Smith, 1964), 127.

58. Cox, "How Judge Hoar Ceased to be Attorney General," 165.

59. Current et al., *The Essentials of American History*, 175.

60. Tansill, *The United States and Santo Domingo*, 340–41.

61. Smith to Seward, 9 March 1869, vol. 6, 2 January 1869–3 June 1871, Despatches from U.S. consuls, T 56/Roll 6.

62. Emilio Rodríguez Demorizi, *Informe de la Comisión de Investigación de los E.U.A. en Santo Domingo en 1871*, vol. 9 of *Academia Dominicana de la Historia*, 10 vols. (Santo Domingo: Montalvo, 1960), 13.

63. Welles, *Naboth's Vineyard*, 1:347, 361.

64. Ibid., 345.

65. Ibid., 361.

66. Ibid., 362. See also Luperón, *Notas Autobiográficas*, 2:113.

67. Smith to Seward, 19 March 1869, vol. 6, T 56/Roll 6.

68. Fabens to Banks, 24 March 1869, Banks Papers.

69. *Hatch Report*, 159.

70. Welles, *Naboth's Vineyard*, 1:365.

71. Ibid., 366.

72. Ibid.

73. Fabens to Fish, 1 April 1869, vol. 2, Notes from the Legations, T 801/Roll 1.

74. Smith to Fish, 9 April 1869, vol. 6, Despatches from U.S. Consuls, T 56/Roll 6.

75. *Boletín Oficial*, second year, no. 104, 19 February 1870, 1. See also Rodman, *Quisqueya*, 115, and Perry to Fish, 7 June 1870, vol. 6, Despatches from U.S. Consuls, T 56/Roll 6.

76. Welles, *Naboth's Vineyard*, 1:359. According to Moya Pons, *Manual de Historia*, 371, the Jesurún (& Zoon) Merchant House loan from Curaçao, which covered the expenses of Báez's return to power in 1868, was later made part of the public debt of the Dominican Republic.

77. Fabens to Fish, 21 April 1869, vol. 2, Notes from the Legations, T 801/Roll 1.

78. Tansill, *The United States and Santo Domingo*, 347.

79. Ibid. Moya Pons, *Manual de Historia*, 373, states that Hartmont was in the Dominican Republic as a result of contact made by allies of Báez in the Jesurún Merchant House, who had earlier unsuccessfully sought money for Báez in the United States.

80. Tansill, *The United States and Santo Domingo*, 347–49. See also Logan, *Haiti and the Dominican Republic*, 45; Peguero and de los Santos, *Visión General*, 230; Moya Pons, *Manual de Historia*, 373–75.

81. Logan, *Haiti and the Dominican Republic*, 45.

82. Ibid., 50.

83. Tansill, *The United States and Santo Domingo*, 355.

84. Smith to Fish, 18 May 1869, vol. 6, Despatches from U.S. Consuls, T 56/Roll 6.

85. Ibid. The Dominican Republic was not the only nation to dangle a potential naval base before the United States. President Salnave of Haiti pretended to offer to cede Môle St. Nicolas to the United States. However, the U.S. consul believed that it was a trick to gain U.S. sympathy. See Arthur Folsom to Fish, 25 July 1869, vol. 10, 31 January 1867–29 December 1869, Despatches from United States Consuls in Cap Haitien 1797–1906, M 9/Roll 9.

86. Tansill, *The United States and Santo Domingo*, 356. See also Welles, *Naboth's Vineyard*, 1:364, for a description of the character of government under Ulysses S. Grant.

87. Tansill, *The United States and Santo Domingo*, 356. See also Joseph W. Fabens to Nathaniel P. Banks, 1 June 1869, Banks Papers.

88. Luperón, *Notas Autobiográficas*, 126–28. See also Moya Pons, *Manual de Historia*, 374.

89. Welles, *Naboth's Vineyard*, 1:368. Peguero and de los Santos, *Visión General*, 214.

90. Moya Pons, *Manual de Historia*, 374, and Welles, *Naboth's Vineyard*, 1:363–64.

91. Fish to Benjamin Hunt, 2 June 1869, Vol. 2, Diplomatic Instructions, M 77/Roll 153.

92. Hunt to Fish, 10 June 1869, vol. 6, Despatches from U.S. Consuls, T 56/Roll 6. See also Tansill, *The United States and Santo Domingo*, 357.

93. Tansill, *The United States and Santo Domingo*, 346–47.

94. Ibid., 357.

95. Ibid., 357–58.

96. Smith to Fish, 22 June 1869, vol. 6, Despatches from U.S. Consuls, T 56/Roll 6.

97. Tansill, *The United States and Santo Domingo*, 358.

98. Gautier to Fabens, 22 June 1869, vol. 2, Notes from the Legations, T 801/Roll 1.

99. Joseph W. Fabens to Charles Sumner, 1 July 1869, Charles Sumner Papers, MS, Houghton Library, Harvard University.

100. Fabens to Fish, 9 July 1869, vol. 2, Notes from the Legations, T 801/Roll 1.

101. Welles, *Naboth's Vineyard*, 1:370.

102. Tansill, *The United States and Santo Domingo*, 351. See also Jesse R. Grant, *In the Days of My Father, General Grant* (New York: Harper Brothers Publishers, 1925), 119–20; The numbers of self-seekers who surrounded Grant reached substantial proportions. See Tansill, *The United States and Santo Domingo*, 350–51. Also see Welles, *Naboth's Vineyard*, 1:364–65; Cox, "How Judge Hoar Ceased to Be Attorney General," 166; Cornelius Cole, *Memoirs* (New York: McLoughlin Brothers, 1908), 324; John Bigelow, *Retrospections of an Active Life*, 4 vols. (Garden City, N.Y.: Doubleday, Page and Co., 1913), 4:306.

103. Fish to Orville Babcock, 13 July 1869, vol. 3, 11 September 1852–31 August 1886, Diplomatic Instructions, M 77/Roll 153.

104. *Hatch Report*, 38. See also Moya Pons, *Manual de Historia*, 374; Gimbernard, *Historia de Santo Domingo*, 234, observes that while Luperón was commencing sea-based activities, Cabral was causing so much trouble on land that Báez was forced to use most of his troops against him. See also Diary of Hamilton Fish, 29 January 1870, MS, Library of Congress, Washington, D.C. Hereafter cited as Fish Diary.

105. *Hatch Report*, 38–39.

106. Ibid., 35–36, 138–39.

107. Ibid., 35–36.

108. Tansill, *The United States and Santo Domingo*, 362. See also Henry M. Wriston, *Executive Agents in American Foreign Relations* (Baltimore: Johns Hopkins University Press, 1929), 164–65.

109. *Hatch Report*, 188–89.

110. Smith to Fish, 2 September 1869, vol. 6, Despatches from U.S. Consuls, T 56/Roll 6.

111. Babcock left the Dominican Republic on 6 September 1869, according to Tansill, *The United States and Santo Domingo*, 363–64. For a colorful description of Babcock's report to Grant, see Cox, "How Judge Hoar Ceased to be Attorney General," 165–67.

112. This irregularity is evident by looking at Article 2, Section 2 [2] of the constitution. See also Cox, "How Judge Hoar Ceased to be Attorney General" and Ellis P. Oberholtzer, *A History of the United States Since the Civil War*, 5 vols. (New York: MacMillan, 1922), 2:230. A version of Babcock's actions in which his signing of the treaty outline is deemed not proper is found in Charles F. Adams, *Lee at Appomattox and Other Papers*, 2d ed. (Boston: Houghton Mifflin and Co., 1902), 131. Tansill, *The United States and Santo Domingo*, 366–70, and Wriston, *Executive Agents*, 164–165, disagree, saying that Babcock was aware that he had only signed a

working draft of what would later be negotiated as a treaty.

113. Oberholtzer, *A History of the United States,* 2:230. Fish more than likely was not surprised at all by Babcock's revelations. See *Hatch Report,* 46–47, and Tansill, *The United States and Santo Domingo,* 367n. In any event Fish was extremely loyal to Grant, being the only member of Grant's cabinet to remain during both of his terms as president. See Badeau, *Grant in Peace,* 231.

114. Badeau, *Grant in Peace,* 231; Oberholtzer, *A History of the United States,* 2:230.

115. Tansill, *The United States and Santo Domingo,* 370.

116. DeBenneville R. Keim, *Santo Domingo* (Philadelphia: Claxton, Remsen & Haffelfinger, 1870), 65–76.

117. Tansill, *The United States and Santo Domingo,* 370. See also Keim to Báez, 16 September 1869, and Báez to Keim, 10 October 1869, DeBenneville R. Keim Papers, MS, Library of Congress, Washington, D.C.

118. Tansill, *The United States and Santo Domingo,* 370.

119. Bernardo Pichardo, *Resumen de Historia Patria,* 5th ed. (Santo Domingo: Colección Pensamiento Dominicana, 1969), 206. Also see Mariano Lebrón Saviñón, *Historia de la Cultura Dominicana,* 2 vols. (Santo Domingo: Publicaciones de Universidad Nacional de Pedro Henríquez Ureña, 1981), 2:142–44.

120. Orville Babcock to Hamilton Fish, 20 October 1869, Ulysses S. Grant Papers, MS, Library of Congress, Washington, D.C.

121. Tansill, *The United States and Santo Domingo,* 372–73.

122. Ibid., 370.

123. Perry to Fish, 7 June 1870, vol. 6, Despatches from U.S. Consuls, T 56/Roll 6.

124. Tansill, *The United States and Santo Domingo,* 371.

125. *U.S. Congress, Senate Executive Document No. 17,* 41st Cong., 3d sess., 16 January 1871 (vol. 1, serial 1440), 80–89.

126. Ibid., 94.

127. Ibid., 94–95.

128. Tansill, *The United States and Santo Domingo,* 373.

129. Ibid., 373–74.

130. Ibid., 375.

131. Perry to Fish, 10 December 1869, vol. 6, Despatches from U.S. Consuls, T 56/Roll 6.

132. Perry to Fish, 7 June 1870, ibid.

133. *Hatch Report,* 49.

134. Perry to Fish, 7 June 1870, vol. 6, Despatches from U.S. Consuls, T 56/Roll 6.

135. *Hatch Report,* 51–52.

136. José Gabriel García, *Historia Moderna de la República Dominicana,* in *Compendio de la Historia de Santo Domingo,* 4 vols., 3d ed. (Santo Domingo: Imprenta de García Hermanos, 1906), 4:187. See also *Hatch Report,* 110.

137. Perry to Fish, 7 June 1870, vol. 6, Despatches from U.S. Consuls, T 56/Roll 6.

138. *Hatch Report,* 110.

139. Ibid. Also Fish Diary, 17 June 1871 and 21 June 1871. See also Hamilton Fish to Elihu Washburne, 24 December 1869, Elihu Washburne Papers, MS, Library of Congress, Washington, D.C.

140. "Note to the Consulting Senate of the Dominican Republic," 29 November 1869, vol. 2, Notes from the Legations, T 801/Roll 1.

141. Perry to Fish, 10 December 1869, vol. 6, Despatches from U.S. Consuls, T 56/Roll 6. See also García, *Compendio de la Historia,* 4:182–83.

142. *Hatch Report,* 110.

143. Ibid. Also Fish Diary, 17 June 1871 and 21 June 1871. See also Hamilton Fish to Elihu Washburne, 24 December 1869, Washburne Papers.

144. *Hatch Report*, 110.

145. Perry to Fish, 10 December 1869, vol. 6, Despatches from U.S. Consuls, T 56/Roll 6. See also García, *Compendio de la Historia*, 4:182–83.

146. Moya Pons, *Manual de Historia*, 376; Tansill, *The United States and Santo Domingo*, 274, 346.

147. García, *Compendio de la Historia*, 4:183, 192–93.

148. Gregorio Luperón and José M. Cabral to the American People, 9 December 1869, vol. 2, T 801/Roll 1. See also Rodríguez Demorizi, *Informe de la Comisión*, 11.

149. Báez to Babcock, 3 December 1869, vol. 2, Notes from the Legations, T 801/Roll 1.

150. Tansill, *The United States and Santo Domingo*, 380–81. See Fish Diary, 21 December 1869.

151. Tansill, *The United States and Santo Domingo*, 382.

152. Perry to Fish, 28 December 1869, vol. 6, Despatches from U.S. Consuls, T 56/Roll 6.

153. Fish to Washburne, 24 December 1869, Washburne Papers.

154. Tansill, *The United States and Santo Domingo*, 381.

155. *New York Herald*, 22 December 1869, 3.

156. Peter F. Stout to Sumner, 24 December 1869, Sumner Papers.

157. Tansill, *The United States and Santo Domingo*, 383.

158. Logan, *Haiti and the Dominican Republic*, 45.

159. Tansill, *The United States and Santo Domingo*, 384–88.

160. Ibid., 386.

161. Daniel Ammen, *The Old Navy and the New* (Philadelphia: J. B. Lippincott Co., 1891), 508. See also *Boston Morning Journal*, 24 October 1877, 2, and Tansill, *The United States and Santo Domingo*, 384–88.

162. Ibid., 386–87.

163. Ibid., 341.

164. Fabens to Fish, 30 December 1869, vol. 2, Notes from the Legations, T 801/Roll 1.

165. *Boston Morning Journal*, 24 October 1877, 2.

166. Fish Diary, 7 January 1870.

167. Richardson, *Messages and Papers of Presidents*, 7:45–46.

168. *New York Herald*, 9 January 1870, 6.

169. Fish Diary, 15 January 1870.

170. Perry to Fish, 20 January 1870, vol. 6, Despatches from U.S. Consuls, T 56/Roll 6.

171. García, *Compendio de la Historia*, 4:187. See also Welles, *Naboth's Vineyard*, 1:382–83, and Peguero and de los Santos, *Visión General*, 232. According to Hazard, *Santo Domingo*, 433, Cabral received $5,000 in gold for his efforts.

172. Tansill, *The United States and Santo Domingo*, 392.

173. Fish Diary, 29 January 1870. See also Rodríguez Demorizi, *Informe de la Comisión*, 20.

174. Tansill, *The United States and Santo Domingo*, 393.

175. Max Henríquez Ureña, *Los Yanquis en Santo Domingo* (Madrid: Imp. de J. Pueyo, 1929), 18. See also "Petition to the American People," 7 February 1870, vol. 2, T 801/Roll 1. See also "Proclama a los Dominicanos, Curaçao 18 de Marzo de 1870," *Boletín del Archivo General de la Nación* 23 (November–December 1960): 8–9. This proclamation, signed by prominent Dominicans and addressed mainly to Dominicans, is against annexation.

176. *New York Tribune*, 5 April 1871, 5, preserves the following quote: "During

the conversation, Mr. Sumner asked Fabens if he thought that annexation would stop with Santo Domingo. 'Oh, no!' replied the Dominican envoy, 'you must have Hayti too.' 'And is that all?' continued the Senator. Fabens thought that we could not stop with Hayti, but must, in the nature of things, finally absorb Porto Rico, Jamaica, Cuba, the Windward Islands, and, indeed, all of the West Indies. Mr. Sumner then called the attention of Fabens to the fact that the treaty involved not only the question of the annexation of the little republic of Santo Domingo, but an entirely new foreign policy of the United States."

177. Charles Callan Tansill, "War Powers of the President," *Political Science Quarterly* 45 (March 1930): 41–44.

178. Fish Diary, 29 April and 3 May 1870; see also Tansill, *The United States and Santo Domingo*, 394.

179. Tansill, *The United States and Santo Domingo*, 395.

180. Perry to Fish, 8 February and 7 June 1870, vol. 6, Despatches from U.S. Consuls, T 56/Roll 6.

181. Tansill, *The United States and Santo Domingo*, 397.

182. Perry to Fish, 20 February 1870, vol. 6, Despatches from U.S. Consuls, T 56/Roll 6.

183. Ibid., 7 June 1870. See also García, *Compendio de la Historia*, 4:187; Moya Pons, *Manual de Historia*, 375; and Gimbernard, *Historia de Santo Domingo*, 235.

184. Gautier to David Coën, 17 March 1870, vol. 2, Notes from the Legations, T 801/Roll 1. See also Gautier to Fish, 19 March 1870, ibid.

185. Gautier to Perry, 9 March 1870, vol. 6, Despatches from U.S. Consuls, T 56/Roll 6. See also Charles H. Poor to George M. Robeson, 12 March 1870, ibid.

186. Rodríguez Demorizi, *Informe de la Comisión*, 23.

187. Tansill, *The United States and Santo Domingo*, 401.

188. Gautier to Perry, 3 May 1870, vol. 6, Despatches from U.S. Consuls, T 56/Roll 6. See also William L. Cazneau to Perry, 4 and 6 May 1870, ibid.

189. Perry to Fish, 11 July 1870, ibid.

190. García, *Compendio de la Historia*, 4:187.

191. Richardson, *Messages and Papers of Presidents*, 7:50.

6

The Saving of the Republic

De cualquier yagua vieja sale un tremendo alacrán.

(There is a rotten apple in every bunch.)

—Dominican proverb

As the spring of 1870 approached, Secretary Fish must have questioned the wisdom of his strategy of looking the other way while Grant pursued Dominican annexation. Already a U.S. citizen had been jailed, one commercial agent was forced out of his post, another was highly disgruntled, and serious constitutional questions had been raised about presidential prerogatives when Grant impulsively sent warships to Dominican waters. In addition, Fish had been forced to mislead his dear friend Charles Sumner, and as this annexation fight wore on, he came very close to making an enemy out of the senator from Massachusetts.

The annexation of the Dominican Republic was now a top priority of the president. It was as if Grant wanted future schoolchildren to read, "The United States expanded its territory to include the Caribbean Islands, starting with initiatives taken by President Ulysses S. Grant when he annexed the Dominican Republic in 1870." Fish probably could not have done anything about it at that time, even if he had wanted to. On 14 March 1870 Grant sent a message to the Senate that the annexation treaty to make the Dominican Republic part of United States territory had been signed on 29 November 1869 and that the time for the exchange of ratifications would expire 29 March 1870. He expressed his wish that he hoped the treaty would not expire by limitation.[1]

At this time Grant was guilty of two fundamental misunderstandings. The first was an indication of his disregard for diplomatic procedure. At the next cabinet meeting Fish told Grant that he was disappointed that by sending the 14 March message to Congress without consulting him, the president was indicating a lack of confidence in the State Department. Although Grant apologized for the oversight and blamed it on his secretary, similar slights would occur in the future.[2] Grant's second misunderstanding was far more profound and ultimately resulted in the failure of the treaty. Although the treaty was never popular with the North American people, Grant, swayed by visions of grandeur and influenced by propaganda, could never understand this basic fact. He equated his own enthusiasm with that of the North American people. If he had grasped the differences between his desires and those of his fellow citizens he might have been able to map out a strategy to convince the U.S. public that the annexation of the Dominican Republic was in its best interests.[3]

On 16 March 1870 the Senate Committee on Foreign Relations reacted negatively to the treaty.[4] Grant, his mind perhaps somewhere between the utterances of Fabens and the new, enlarged map of the United States he may have been envisioning, became extremely angry. True to military form, he went on the attack immediately by rushing to the Hill with Babcock, bringing along the necessary props that supposedly would convince skeptics.[5] Perhaps it was understandable that a man like Grant would find it incredulous that anyone could fail to see the boon to the United States that would come with the passage of the treaty. He was in a sense a North American *caudillo* trapped in a political system that demanded alternative forms of persuasion.

It had been easy for Báez to order a rigged referendum and then pronounce the country as eager for annexation. When Manuel Gautier wrote, "Great is the desire prevailing in the country at large for annexation to the United States,"[6] he was talking about the result of a plebiscite in which dissention was simply not tolerated. Although Grant was not able to engage in the same sort of persuasive activities in the United States, he did know that he was dealing with a legislative opposition—and so he set out to pressure politically those who would be called upon to vote on the treaty. As Senator Sumner said at a later stage in the struggle:

> On another occasion I showed how these wrongful proceedings had been sustained by the President beyond all example but in a corresponding spirit. Never before has there been such Presidential intervention in the Senate as we have been constrained to witness. Presidential visits to the Capitol, with appeals to Senators, have been followed by assemblies at the Executive Mansion, also with appeals to Senators, and who can measure the pressure of all kinds by himself or agents, especially through the appointing power, all to secure the consummation of this scheme.[7]

Senator Charles Sumner. *(Courtesy of Perkins Library, Duke University.)*

Although it may be obvious that Senator Sumner was biased, his observations had been borne out by the resignation of cabinet members, the forced resignations of the minister to Great Britain and Perry, and certainly by the eventual fate of Sumner himself.

On 24 March 1870 the debate on the treaty of annexation began in the Senate. Grant and his partisans were already at a disadvantage because Sumner had made an opposition speech in which his views on the treaty were those that had little to do with antipathy toward Grant but rather revolved around several logical points that would have to be considered on their own merits:

a) The proposed annexation would probably encourage further American acquisitions of Caribbean territory and would thus involve the United

States in serious complications with other powers. b) There was little likelihood of further intervention by European powers in the affairs of the Dominican Republic. c) The United States, in the event of annexation, would probably be saddled with a public debt much larger than had been anticipated. d) Continued civil war and rebellions would be the aftermath of annexation. e) Annexation would impair the predominance of the colored race in the West Indies and therefore would be unjust to it.[8]

The annexationists were now under some additional pressures. They would have to show how the proposed annexation of the Dominican Republic would benefit someone other than William L. Cazneau, Joseph W. Fabens, Buenaventura Báez, and Ulysses S. Grant.[9]

This task apparently fell on the shoulders of Senator Oliver P. Morton of Indiana. To Morton the Dominican Republic was a virgin wilderness, without people or technology, just waiting for North American guidance.[10] As Morton spoke at the debate, Babcock hovered in the wings and at various junctures in the proceedings exhibited wares and mineral samples from the Dominican Republic.[11] This ploy was unsuccessful, for after speeches by other senators the treaty expired by limitation on 29 March 1870.[12] It may have surprised Grant, but there was little public outcry in the United States after the expiration of the treaty. At that time there were probably far more Ku Klux Klan meetings going on than rallies demanding Dominican annexation. The one public meeting that had attracted considerable attention was held on 12 May 1870 in New York City. Although the selected speaker failed to appear, this rally nevertheless was a testimonial to the level of propaganda of which the proannexationists were capable. Speakers pointed out that the Dominican Republic had not only vast quantities of gold but that its acquisition would leave "the American Continent to the American people."[13]

In the Dominican Republic, Báez, who had learned that a group of foreign merchants had contributed eight thousand dollars to assist Cabral and Luperón,[14] was extremely disappointed with the outcome of the treaty debates in the U.S. Congress. He could take some comfort in the fact that in preparing for this eventuality, he had, on 16 April 1870, authorized Colonel Fabens to go to Washington as the Dominican envoy extraordinary and minister plenipotentiary to try to arrange some sort of U.S. aid.[15] Báez was also relieved to see the continued presence of U.S. naval vessels in Dominican waters. In fact, the commander of one had gone so far as to deliver ultimatums to the Haitian government.[16]

Fabens arrived at the State Department for a conference with Secretary Fish. He made the same mistake of visiting Grant before seeing Fish and once again had to be rescued by the president.[17] Eventually, on 14 May 1870, Fish signed an article extending until 1 July 1870 the time for exchange of ratifications.[18] Fabens had not achieved his initial objective of procuring funds for Báez's bankrupt government.[19] On the other hand, he had been able to rescue the treaty by extending the time needed for exchange of ratifications. Note the following correspondence, written by Fabens to Cazneau in the period between his meetings with Fish and the deadline for exchange of ratifications:

> President Grant is fully determined on the annexation of Santo Domingo, and *he will succeed*. . . . I have had a four hours interview with Sumner and have good grounds for hoping that he will come around. He evidently sees his mistake and laments it. Prest. Grant [*sic*] proposes next week to meet him with me, and I think we have an argument that will convert him. But *with or without him* we intend to succeed, and if the situation remains unchanged in Santo Domingo we shall succeed.[20]

Meanwhile, Major Perry was due to arrive in Washington from the Dominican Republic. He had recently seen to it that Davis Hatch was safely on the way to Cuba; he had witnessed severe obstruction of the freedom to express opinions in the Dominican plebiscite of the past February; he had sat quietly by as an annexation treaty was negotiated in an atmosphere of bribes; and he slowly had become angry at the way in which Cazneau and Fabens seemed to be influencing not only the Dominican government, but also U.S. officials. On 1 June 1870 Perry personally called on Secretary Fish. According to the major, Cazneau and Fabens were reckless speculators who not only tried to monopolize all manner of concessions in the Dominican Republic, but attempted to subvert the interests of President Grant in favor of their own.[21] Judging by the reactions of Fish about Fabens in the past, it is likely that Fish concurred with Perry's accountings—but Fish was not Grant's supervisor. As for Grant, one can surmise that even he by now was aware that his confederates in the Dominican Republic were not spotless. However, Grant considered the question of colonial expansion too important for quibbling about the ethics of one's agents in the field. The main objective was the acquisition of the Dominican Republic. Later there would be time for niceties such as the morals of subordinates. Báez's thinking ran much the same way. His chief goal was the protection of the United States. This, of course, would neutralize the interference of the Haitians and also bring in hordes of North Americans. Undoubtedly Báez also knew with whom he was dealing among the U.S. proannexationists in the Dominican Republic, but he was perfectly willing to be used in order to get what he wanted.

In any event, Grant was not going to let the possibly biased utterances of a one-time mule thief (according to Fish[22]) stand in the way of territorial expansion. Within the last two weeks Grant had already spoken to Congress twice, endorsing the annexation of the Dominican Republic. The benefits he described were extensive and varied, from building up the merchant marine and paying off the national debt to national security and the abolition of slavery in Cuba, Puerto Rico, and Brazil.[23] He also tried to scare Congress into supporting annexation because he had "reliable evidence" that a European power was willing to pay "two million dollars for Samaná Bay alone."[24]

The plan did not work. Opponents of annexation were not won over and, perhaps more important, there seemed to be no public pressure to turn their opinions. In fact, rather than receiving a swell of support for the treaty, Grant had to countenance the Senate hearings on the imprisonment of Davis Hatch, which were occurring in June 1870.[25] At this time the Senate was receiving letters from such noteworthy Dominican exiles as Mariano A. Cestero and José Gabriel García, a prominent historian.[26] It now seemed obvious to Grant that the pressure would have to be increased. He reasoned that a unified cabinet would send a signal to recalcitrant senators that his administration was determined to push through this treaty. On 13 June 1870 Grant complained to Fish that the cabinet was not supporting him unanimously on the treaty.[27] Just before this conversation Fish had been the recipient of a visit from Senator Cornelius Cole, "Judge" Peter J. O'Sullivan, and Colonel Fabens. In their own ways, each had tried to secure from Fish some manner of financial assistance for Báez's destitute government. A horrified Fish had replied that to allow Báez to borrow anything would be a violation of the terms of the treaty. Fabens then had informed Fish that he had a letter from the Hartmont Company that asserted that their loan was valid and would have to be carried out, but that the company would be willing to accept a lease of Samaná for fifty years.[28]

Fish had shown no interest in these proposals[29] and now he replied to the president that the secretary of the treasury was not in favor of the treaty but that he did not know of any others who had spoken negatively on annexation.[30] On the following day Grant met his cabinet and told them that he expected all members to support the treaty. Although most generally approved of the treaty,[31] there were a few who did not. The cabinet member most outwardly negative seemed to be the attorney general, Judge Ebenezer R. Hoar. Within less than a day Hoar sent Grant his resignation, which Grant immediately accepted.[32] Jacob D. Cox, secretary of the interior, was to go later, and Fish continued to make sporadic attempts at resigning.[33]

With the cabinet now in line, it was time for Grant to deal with wayward senators. The day was fast approaching when the treaty would expire, and the president needed a favorable vote, which he did not get the first time. Because Senator Sumner had been the most visible opponent of the treaty,[34] it seemed most reasonable that Grant make an example of him by punishment. In a conversation with proannexation senators in June 1870, Grant was told that senators who opposed the annexation treaty apparently received more patronage than those who supported it. Grant answered by saying that this situation would change, starting with Sumner, who had been responsible for the appointment of John L. Motley as minister to Great Britain.[35] On 28 June, Grant discussed with Fish and others the question of Motley's removal. It seems evident that Grant's disapproval of the scholarly Motley was not based on Motley's job performance.[36]

On 29 June 1870 the debate in the Senate over annexation of the Dominican Republic started up again. Sumner did not speak at all but the vote nevertheless ended in a tie—short of the two-thirds majority vote needed for ratification.[37] Grant, a Republican, had now suffered the first major legislative defeat of his administration. He immediately struck back at Sumner by ordering the removal of Motley,[38] but he just as well could have blamed the U.S. general public. Again, there were no significant protests. The fact that the president had put so much of his office's prestige on the line should have been enough to result in the treaty's passage, but the numbers of North Americans who wanted the Dominican Republic as a territory were just not there.

Possibly Báez was not immediately concerned with the outcome of the Senate vote, in spite of his government's financial problems, because even as late as the beginning of 1871 the United States was still giving him direct military protection.[39] In August 1870, however, he was forced to write Grant a letter of inquiry on the Dominican annexation. Grant, not wanting to disappoint the Dominican leader any more than necessary, replied some weeks later that he still held out hopes that the United States could annex the Dominican Republic and that, when Congress convened, he would send to that body another message recommending annexation.[40] This must have spurred Báez to continue the fight, for a few weeks later Colonel Fabens wrote Fish that, as minister plenipotentiary from the president of the Dominican Republic, he had the authority to make a new treaty of annexation.[41] Fabens quickly followed this letter up with a visit to the State Department but was told by Fish that his credentials only gave him power to negotiate a treaty of annexation. Since the treaty of annexation had since expired, Fabens's credentials were worthless.[42]

Once again, however, Grant came to the aid of the colonel, for while Fish was thoroughly embarrasing Fabens, Grant had sent—on 5 December 1870—a message to Congress recommending a joint resolution authorizing the president to appoint a joint commission to negotiate a treaty with Dominican authorities for the acquisition of that island.[43] The reference Grant made to "that island" perhaps explains the enthusiastic support of the Haitians to Blue leaders fighting Báez and the activities of Preston, the Haitian minister to the United States. On opposite sides of the annexation fight, the parties sprung into action, using different methods. On 9 December 1870 W. M. Ringwood, a member of the firm of Spofford, Tileston and Company, wrote to Fabens to inform him that he would have plenty of money to buy the votes necessary for success in Congress.[44] On the same day, Senator Sumner introduced into the Senate a resolution demanding that the president send it "all papers and correspondence relating to the proposed annexation of the Dominican portion of the island of Santo Domingo."[45]

This was the last chance for annexation short of an illegal filibuster of the type carried out by William Walker in Nicaragua.[46] At this time Republican allies of Grant's administration became concerned that no additional defeats be recorded against their president. In this group are those to whom the Dominican Republic had little meaning. The presidency of Grant, after all, signified far more than a mere presidential administration. As a Republican symbolizing a philosophy that contrasted to strongly held beliefs in the South and throughout the nation, Grant was a president who was under pressure in more ways than one. His allies in the Senate rallied to his side and on 12 December 1870 Senator Morton introduced a resolution allowing the president to appoint three commissioners to proceed to the Dominican Republic for the purpose of surveying the political, social, and economic conditions present. In their report they also were to ascertain whether the people of the Dominican Republic wanted to be annexed to the United States. Presumably this would also be the committee that would negotiate the acquisition of the Dominican Republic to the United States.[47] The opponents of annexation countered with a motion that this resolution should be referred to the Senate Committee on Foreign Relations, which Morton did not want to happen because of the presumed influence of Sumner on that committee.[48] As the debate ensued the Senate had the occasion to witness the 21 December 1870 speech of Senator Sumner against the resolution:

> The resolution before the Senate commits Congress to a dance of blood. It is a new step in a measure of violence. Already several steps have been taken and Congress is now summoned to another. The Senator, it seems to me, has not comprehended the object of this resolution. To my mind it is plain. The object of the resolution, and I will demonstrate it, is to commit Congress to the policy of annexation. . . . I use strong language, but only what the occason [sic] requires. As senator, as a patriot, I cannot see my country suffer in its good name without an earnest effort to save it. . . . The Island of San Domingo, situated in tropical waters and occupied by another race, can never become a permanent possession of the United States. You may seize it by force of arms or by diplomacy, where an able squadron does more than the Minister, but the enforced jurisdiction cannot endure. It is theirs by right of possession; by their sweat and blood mingling with the soil; by tropical position; by its burning sun and the unalterable laws of climate. Such is the ordinance of nature which I am not the first to recognize. San Domingo is the earliest of that independent group destined to occupy the Caribbean Sea toward which our duty is plain as the Ten Commandments. Kindness, benevolence, assistance, aid, help, protection, all that is implied in good neighborhood, this we must give freely, bountifully; but their independence is as precious to them as is ours to us and it is placed under the safeguard of natural laws which we cannot violate with impunity.[49]

Sumner unwisely embellished his earlier logical statements with some personal attacks on Báez, Cazneau, Fabens, and Babcock. However, he had the foresight to criticize Grant's use of the U.S. navy in implementing his annexation policy.[50] He was joined by Senator Carl Schurz, who did not believe in tropical expansion,[51] perhaps because of his German background. Nevertheless, in spite of a lengthy debate laden with threats, insults, and innuendo,[52] the Morton resolution passed the Senate on 21 December 1870 by the vote of 32 to 9.[53] Later the resolution was taken up in the House, where Congressman Jacob Ambler introduced an amendment stating that the resolution before them should not be interpreted as committing the United States to a policy of annexation of the Dominican Republic.[54] The amendment was supported and the resolution, with the amendment, was passed on 10 January 1871 by a vote of 123 to 63.[55] On 11 January 1870 the Senate unanimously concurred with the Ambler amendment.[56] The president approved the joint resolution on 12 January 1871 and appointed his commission immediately: members were Dr. Samuel G. Howe, a well-known philanthropist, former Senator Benjamin F. Wade, and Andrew D. White, Cornell University president.[57] The commission promptly left the United States on 17 January 1871.[58] However, even before they had been formally appointed, Colonel Fabens had made preparations for the commissioners. In a letter dated 31 December 1870 to Manuel Gautier, Fabens implied that the commission itself would be subject to his influences.[59] In addition to their stated mission of fact-finding and their projected involvement with Colonel Fabens and his clique, the commission had one other task. Tansill describes it:

> Before the departure of the commission from the United States, President Grant had indicated his desire that the members examine most carefully the town records in the Dominican Republic for any evidence that he or any other American official had received any concessions of any kind from the Dominican government.[60]

This additional task was advisable because Sumner, during the fall of 1870, had indicated that Grant himself was seeking financial gain from the annexation of the Dominican Republic.[61]

The commission arrived in the Dominican Republic on 24 January 1871 and began their investigation.[62] The commission subsequently found no evidence of Grant receiving any financial gain from the proposed annexation.[63] The presence of Cazneau and Fabens was felt during the stay of the commissioners. An associate of Fabens, "Professor" William L. Gabb, took upon himself the task of making sure that the education of the commissioners followed the right lines.[64] The validity of what Gabb told the members of the commission can be surmised from the fact that Gabb himself had extensive holdings in the Dominican Republic.[65] Buenaventura Báez himself was called upon to display his charm and at least two commissioners were favorably impressed with the Dominican chief executive:

> Báez was a man of force and ability, and, though a light mulatto, he had none of the characteristics generally attributed in the United States to men of mixed blood. He had rather the appearance of a swarthy Spaniard, and in all of his conduct he showed quiet self-reliance, independence, and the tone of a high-spirited gentleman. . . . There was a quiet elegance in his manners and conversation which would have done credit to any statesman in any country, and he had gathered about him as his cabinet two or three really superior men who appeared devoted to his fortunes. I have never doubted that his overtures to General Grant were patriotic.[66]

Further:

> He is simple and courteous in manners; has considerable culture; and is familiar with European countries and languages. He is respected and

beloved by his neighbors, who are very proud of him, as I can testify. He has been much abroad, and is there regarded as an able diplomat.[67]

Obviously influenced by proannexationist sentiment, the commission returned to the United States on 26 March 1871 with a favorable report. According to the commission, the Domincan people were healthy, uneducated but educable, unencumbered but desiring annexation with the United States, and possessing a land that was extremely fertile.[68] The voices that had expressed doubts about the Dominican president and the supposed riches of the Dominican Republic did not find their way into the thinking of the commissioners or their report.[69]

While the commission had been in the Dominican Republic, Grant had been busy trying to neutralize Sumner. Finally he was able to remove Sumner from the position of chair of the Senate Committee on Foreign Relations. He first used the pretext that Sumner no longer had a personal relationship with the president. When that rationale became too transparent. Grant's Senate allies cited the reasons below:

1) Sumner was negligent in not reporting treaties referred to the Senate Committee on Foreign Relations. 2) He was seriously at fault in not "moving forward" the treaties in the Senate and "securing its action upon them." 3) He would have impeded the negotiation and ratification of the Treaty of Washington.[70]

This onslaught did little to impede Sumner from preparing a speech opposing Grant's annexation policy, which he gave on 27 March 1871, before the arrival in the capital of the commissioners from the Dominican Republic. In this famous speech Sumner centered his criticism of Grant's actions on the president's use of the navy to provide protection for the Dominican government while the treaty negotiations were going on. Such actions, he said, violated the war powers of Congress.[71] This viewpoint was seconded by Senator Carl Schurz in a lively debate between Schurz and Senator Timothy O. Howe on 28 March 1871:

Mr. Schurz: What is that great safeguard of our peace and security, as it is written in the Constitution, that Congress, and not the President alone shall have the power to declare war—what is it worth if an executive officer of the Government can initiate or make war without congressional authority? . . .

Mr. Howe: If my friend will allow me, he did not understand what I said, but he evidently misunderstands what I intended by it. I simply said that the President could, in the discharge of his authority over the Army and Navy, commit an act of war. I did not say he could rightfully do it,

Senator Carl Schurz. *(Courtesy of the Library of Congress.)*

but I said he would be amenable to our Government for any such conduct.

Mr. Schurz: That is another thing.

Mr. Howe: I was only trying to make a distinction between an act of war and a declaration of war.

Mr. Schurz: Very well; let us lay down the meaning of the constitutional provision in these terms: that the executive department of the Government shall not commit an act of war except in the case of an invasion of the United States by a foreign enemy, unless expressly authorized by Congress. Is that it? . . . I therefore affirm that the President in ordering the naval commanders of the United States to capture and destroy by force of arms the vessels of a nation *whom the United States were at peace,* in a contigency arbitrarily defined by himself other than self-defense, did usurp the war-making power of Congress. [Emphasis added.][72]

Although Senator James Harlan defended Grant's policy by pointing out that on other occasions the U.S. government had deployed military forces without a formal declaration of war by Congress, the impression on the Senate left by Sumner and Schurz was clearly felt. Upon the receipt of the report by the commissioners, President Grant, in a 5 April 1871 message to Congress, indicated that the commissioners' report absolved him and his agents of corruption in regard to the annexation of the Dominican Republic. He therefore was willing to let the North American people decide the Dominican matter.[73] No further positive action was ever taken by Congress with regard to the Dominican Republic's annexation by the United States.[74]

The Dominican Republic had been saved. The central players in this drama would go on to different fates. President Grant was elected to a second term in 1872. His secretary of state, Hamilton Fish, became the only cabinet member in Grant's administration to serve throughout the entire eight years Grant was president.[75]

Senator Sumner, an emotional and deeply sensitive man, had suffered an attack of angina even before the return of the commissioners from the Dominican Republic and died soon after the rejection of the annexation.[76] Cazneau and Fabens, their plans for the Dominican "territory" smashed, would go elsewhere.[77] Báez served almost three more years as Dominican President.[78] He even held office once more later in the decade, again pleading for annexation to the United States[79] and again resorting to duplicity and repression before making his final exit from Dominican politics.[80] Luperón served later as Dominican president before being banished by his protegé, Ulises Heureaux.[81]

The legality of Grant's military assistance to the Dominican Republic while the treaty was being considered for ratification by the U.S. Congress has been debated in both the nineteenth and twentieth centuries. Using two separate rationales, Tansill has challenged the position of Grant in deploying naval forces to the Dominican Republic. According to article 4 of the annexation treaty:

> The people of the Dominican Republic shall, in the shortest possible time, express in a manner conformable to their laws, their will concerning the cession herein provided for; and the United States shall, until such expression shall be had, protect the Dominican Republic against foreign interposition, in order that the national expression may be free.[82]

Báez had held his plebiscite on 19 February 1870 and the results were communicated to the U.S. secretary of state on 19 March 1870. President Grant, in sending orders to deploy naval forces in the West Indies to aid Báez's government after that date, was in violation of that article of the treaty.[83] The only other basis for U.S. protection of the Dominican Republic would have centered around the protection of Samaná. The United States had taken possession of Samaná on the day of the Dominican signing of the treaty of annexation, pending annexation by the United States. Even assuming that U.S. forces had to be deployed to the Dominican Republic to protect the North American presence at Samaná, the final expiration of the treaty in the U.S. Congress on 1 July 1870 should have been the latest date when the Dominican Republic could have received U.S. protection.[84] However, Grant was still issuing orders for Dominican protection well beyond that point.[85] Ironically, Grant had wanted to extend for one year the lease on Samaná in order to allow the exchange of treaty ratifications for annexation to take place as late as 1 July 1871. To do this he had arranged for Colonel Fabens and Secretary Fish to sign an article on 7 July 1870 that extended the time for exchange of ratifications to 1 July 1871. Through an oversight, Grant's article was never received by the Senate, so it was never voted upon.[86]

What happened to the Dominican Republic? The future was not kind to that island nation. Many years of strife, hardship, and brutal dictatorship lay ahead. The long-suffering Dominican people had to cope with the autocratic rule of Ulises "Lilis" Heureaux; the fratricidal battles of the *Jimenistas* and the *Horacistas* after the turn of the century; the American occupation of 1916–24 in which ethnocentric U.S. military officers built roads but trained the constabulary that fostered the rise of Rafael Leonidas Trujillo Molina; and the dictatorship of Trujillo himself, perhaps the most totalitarian dictatorship in Latin American history.[87]

In the eyes of many Dominicans, however, these and other privations have at least been borne by a nation. With a change of a few votes in the U.S. Senate in 1870, this situation would have been changed forever. The struggles for independence in 1844, the War of the Second Independence, and the fight against Báez and his coterie of annexationists helped define and shape Dominican social and political thought. Men such as Hostos and Bonó debated the nature of the Dominican political system;[88] the initiatives of one of Baez's successors, Archbishop Arturo de Meriño, resulted in the immigration of persons from Cuba and Puerto Rico who contributed to the country's intellectual and social base.[89] That the phenomenon of *caudillismo* still existed and would continue to exist in the Dominican Republic is clear: one need only look at the subsequent dictatorships of Heureaux and Trujillo.

The important difference between the *caudillismo* exercised by Pedro Santana and that exemplified by Heureaux and Trujillo, however, is the emergence of a more coherent Dominican nationalism after the annexation struggle. Whatever was said of Trujillo, he nevertheless emphasized the idea of the Dominican nation,[90] whereas Santana had been content to deliver his country to Spain in order to receive a title and a pension.[91] This nationalism was present in the Dominican Republic when the United States occupied the country for the first time in 1916–24. As Bailey and Nasatir describe it:

A direct military government was established under the United States Navy Department. But this direct American rule was not carried out through puppet presidents as was done in Haiti, for the *proud Dominicans* refused to serve as such puppets. The subterfuge was therefore maintained that this was "an independent state under temporary occupation." [Emphasis added.][92]

The conception of nationalism now nascent in the Dominican people may have been the legacy of Buenaventura Báez and his enemies' struggles against his protectionist policies.

Notes

1. Richardson, *Messages and Papers of Presidents*, 7:52–53.
2. Fish Diary, 15 March 1870.
3. Abraham Lincoln was able to transform his fight to save the Union into one that was somehow a "national goal." See Williams, *Empire as a Way of Life*, 92. See also Current et al., *The Essentials of American History*, 153–54.
4. *New York Herald*, 16 March 1870, 3, 6.
5. Tansill, *The United States and Santo Domingo*, 404.
6. Gautier to Fish, 19 March 1870, vol. 2, Notes from the Legations, T 801/Roll 1.

7. *Congressional Globe,* 42d Cong., 1st sess., 27 March 1871, 304.

8. Pierce, *Memoirs and Letters of Charles Sumner,* 4:440–41.

9. Cazneau tried to do just that. See William L. Cazneau, *To the American Press: The Dominican Negotiations* (Santo Domingo: García Hermanos, 1870).

10. *New York Herald,* 26 March 1870, 8; the *New York World,* 25 March 1870, 2, forecast Morton's upcoming presentation.

11. *New York Herald,* 26 March 1870, 8.

12. Tansill, *The United States and Santo Domingo,* 407.

13. *New York Times,* 13 May 1970, 1. Also see Weinstein and Wilson, *Freedom and Crisis,* 1:428, for a brief glimpse of the menace—and popularity—of the Ku Klux Klan at that time.

14. Welles, *Naboth's Vineyard,* 1:387.

15. Tansill, *The United States and Santo Domingo,* 402–3, 412.

16. Perry to Fish, 28 December 1869, vol. 6, Despatches from U.S. Consuls, T 56/Roll 6.

17. Tansill, *The United States and Santo Domingo,* 403.

18. Fish Diary, 14 May 1870.

19. Perry to Fish, 14 May 1870, vol. 6, Despatches from U.S. Consuls, T 56/Roll 6.

20. Fabens to Cazneau, 4 May 1870, cited in Tansill, *The United States and Santo Domingo,* 408n.

21. Fish Diary, 1 June 1870.

22. Ibid., 14 June 1870.

23. Richardson, *Messages and Papers of Presidents,* 7:61–83.

24. Ibid. For an assessment of the veracity of this assertion, see Sir Edward Thornton to Lord Clarendon, 6 June 1870, F.O. 5/1193, No. 248, Public Record Office, London England. Also see Thornton to Clarendon, 13 June 1870. F.O. 5/1193, No. 264, ibid.

25. Tansill, *The United States and Santo Domingo,* 411n.

26. Welles, *Naboth's Vineyard,* 1:395.

27. Tansill, *The United States and Santo Domingo,* 416–17.

28. Fish Diary, 1 June 1870.

29. Ibid.

30. Tansill, *The United States and Santo Domingo,* 417.

31. Fish Diary, 14 June 1870. See also Adams, *Lee at Appomattox,* 218.

32. Ulysses S. Grant to Ebenezer R. Hoar, 15 June 1870, Grant Papers.

33. Tansill, *The United States and Santo Domingo,* 340n.

34. Carl Schurz to W. N. Grosvenor, 31 March 1870, Carl Schurz Papers, MS, Library of Congress; Washington, D.C.

35. Fish Diary, 25 June 1870. Even before Grant had raged against Sumner, saying that he would not let those who opposed him "name ministers to London." See ibid., 14 June 1870.

36. Oliver Wendell Holmes, *John Lothrop Motley* (Boston: Houghton Osgood & Co., 1879), chap. 21.

37. *Journal of the Executive Proceedings of the Senate of the United States,* 41st Cong., 2d sess. (Washington, D.C.: Government Printing Office, 1901), 17:502, 503.

38. Holmes, *John Lothrop Motley.* For a look at Grant's choice of Motley's successor, see W. E. Woodward, *Meet General Grant* (New York: Horace Liveright, 1928), 448.

39. *Senate Executive Document No. 34,* 41st Cong., 3d sess., 7 February 1871,

23–29. Rear Admiral S. P. Lee saw fit to enter the civilian world of political speculation with a verbal blast at annexation opponents. See Ibid., 28.

40. Tansill, *The United States and Santo Domingo*, 427–28. See Fish Diary, 15 October 1870, and Grant to Báez, 17 October 1870, Grant Papers.

41. Fabens to Fish, 6 December 1870, vol. 2, Notes from the Legations, T 801/ Roll 1.

42. Tansill, *The United States and Santo Domingo*, 428–29.

43. Richardson, *Messages and Papers of Presidents*, 7:99–101.

44. Babcock is clearly implicated in these machinations in William M. Ringwood to Joseph W. Fabens, 9 December 1870, cited in Tansill, *The United States and Santo Domingo*, 429.

45. *Congressional Globe*, 41st Cong., 3d sess., 9 December 1870, 51.

46. See p. 42.

47. *Congressional Globe*, 41st Cong., 3d sess., 12 December 1870, 53.

48. Tansill, *The United States and Santo Domingo*, 430.

49. *Congressional Globe*, 41st Congress, 3d sess., 21 December 1870, 226–31. A twentieth-century observation by Betances de Pujadas in *Origen y Proyecciones*, 107, is reminiscent of Sumner's passion. The literal translation is: "It is a shame that in the history of a nation like the United States, where it has served for years as inspiration and example to the democratic life and to the ideal of human rights, pages are registered of the secrecy such as the negotiations with Báez that darkened and miraculously did not annihilate our nation."

50. *Congressional Globe*, 41st Cong., 3d Sess., 21 December 1870, 226–31.

51. Ibid., 255.

52. Ibid., 222–31, 236, 271.

53. Ibid., 271.

54. Ibid., 416.

55. Ibid.

56. Ibid., 431.

57. Grant to Báez, 15 January 1871, Grant Papers.

58. Tansill, *The United States and Santo Domingo*, 436.

59. Moya Pons, *Manual de Historia*, 375. Fabens also linked General Babcock to his plans.

60. Tansill, *The United States and Santo Domingo*, 437–38.

61. *New York Herald*, 21 November 1870, 3.

62. Tansill, *The United States and Santo Domingo*, 436. See also a letter to Manuel Gautier, 8 March 1871, which appeared in "Secciones de Relaciones Exteriores, 1871," *Archivo General de la Nación*, Santo Domingo, R.D. In this letter, Fabens calls Perry, Hatch, and Sumner a triumvirate and praises the commission.

63. *Senate Executive Document No. 9*, 42d Cong., 1st sess., 5 April 1871 (vol. 1, serial 1466), 31.

64. William L. Gabb to Fabens, 11 February 1871, cited in Tansill, *The United States and Santo Domingo*, 437.

65. Boin and Serulle Ramía, *El Proceso de Desarrollo*, 117.

66. Andrew Dickson White, *Autobiography*, 2 vols. (New York: Century Co., 1905), 1:490.

67. Samuel G. Howe, *Letters on the Proposed Annexation of Santo Domingo* (Boston: Wright and Potter, 1871), 14–15.

68. *Senate Executive Document No. 9*, 42d Cong., 1st sess., 5 April 1871 (vol. 1, serial 1466), 1–34. See esp. 23–24 for a discussion of Samaná Bay.

69. Ibid., 144–45. See also *New York Tribune*, 17 March 1871: "They [the Dominican Army] had no standard of their own, but they bore with great pride an

American flag. . . . This was no accident or lawless fancy of the soldiers. Báez has made similar use of false colors before." See also José Gabriel García, *Examen Critico del Informe de los Comisionados de Santo Domingo Dedicado al Pueblo de los Estados Unidos* (Caracas: A. L. S. Muller, C. J. & A. W. Newman, 1871), 1–3, in which García states that the commissioners' informants had altered the truth, that the protest against Báez was essentially a patriotic one, and that the annexationist sentiment was not spontaneous but part of a carefully hatched plot. At about this time another message signed by prominent Dominicans was revealed to have been addressed to the commissioners in February. The message stated that in 1844 Báez was a Haitian, in 1853 he was French, and in 1861 he was Spanish. See "Mensaje a la Comisión de Investigación de E.U.A. en Santo Domingo, Febrero 3 de 1871," *Boletín del Archivo General de la Nación* 23 (January–December 1960): 101–8.

70. Tansill, *The United States and Santo Domingo*, 454.

71. *Congressional Globe*, 42d Cong., 1st sess., 27 March 1871, 294.

72. Ibid., 51–52 (app.).

73. Richardson, *Messages and Papers of Presidents*, 7:130.

74. Welles, *Naboth's Vineyard*, 1:400.

75. See p. 75.

76. Tansill, *The United States and Santo Domingo*, 456, and Welles, *Naboth's Vineyard*, 1:400.

77. Welles, *Naboth's Vineyard*, 1:401.

78. Logan, *Haiti and the Dominican Republic*, 203.

79. Paul Jones to Hamilton Fish, 16 January 1877, vol. 8, 6 January 1874–30 June 1877, Despatches from U.S. Consuls, T 56/Roll 8.

80. Welles, *Naboth's Vineyard*, 1:430; Rodman, *Quisqueya*, 90; Logan, *Haiti and the Dominican Republic*, 47.

81. Rodman, *Quisqueya*, 100.

82. See the Appendix for the entire annexation treaty.

83. Tansill, *The United States and Santo Domingo*, 460–61.

84. Ibid., 463.

85. *Senate Executive Document No. 34*, 41st Cong., 3d sess., 7 February 1871 (vol. 1, serial 1440) 23–29.

86. Fish Diary, 17 June 1871.

87. Crassweller, *Trujillo*.

88. Hoetink, *The Dominican People*, chap. 6.

89. Rodman, *Quisqueya*, 95.

90. Crassweller, *Trujillo*. According to Moya Pons, *Manual de Historia*, 519–21, 524–25, Trujillo based a large part of his propaganda machine on the concept of nationalism and patriotism, which indicates that by then it was an important concept.

91. Logan, *Haiti and the Dominican Republic*, 41.

92. Bailey and Nasatir, *Latin America*, 679.

7

Conclusion

El que nació para guanimo hasta del cielo le caen las hojas.

(If a man is destined for bad luck, he will not escape it.)

—Dominican proverb

One could argue that the only genuine hero in the annexation struggle was Gregorio Luperón, a leader in the fight against Spain in the *Restauración*.[1] A self-made man,[2] he fought against all types of enemies, both Dominican and foreign. An ardent liberal, he refused to accept the constitutional presidency after having served as provisional president in 1880.[3] Significantly, Luperón has been revered by both Dominicans and students of Dominican history.

As for Senator Sumner, a flaw in his personality makes one reluctant to grant him the same status as Luperón. Although Sumner could be called a "friend of the colored man," he fell into the same trap as have many people who fancy themselves racial liberals in twentieth-century United States. Slow to enter into meaningful relationships with most of the people of color with whom he came into contact, he was at the same time capable of a great amount of symbolic concern for colored people.[4] Nevertheless, thanks must go to the Massachusetts senator for serving as the foremost fighter in the United States against the treaty. The Dominicans sending petitions and letters to Sumner certainly knew that he was the leader in the struggle against annexation in the United States.[5] Senator Schurz likewise was an important figure in the antiannexation camp if only for the fact that his statements relieved Sumner of the burden of being an isolated critic of President Grant.

If it were not for the fact that the sovereignty of the Dominican Republic was at stake, the annexation struggle had the makings of a comic opera. Since the annexation of the Dominican Republic was never a real desire of either the North American or Dominican people, the annexation proponents had to somehow subvert the genuine prerogatives of both the United States and the Dominican Republic to fit their aims. For many of the Dominican annexationists, who wanted only to preside over a North American colony that would provide them more money and power, the annexation had to be portrayed as an opportunity to merge the destiny of the Dominican Republic with that of the powerful and respected United States. All too often the Dominican annexationists did not respect opposing views, which resulted in the implementation of repressive measures.

In the United States, faced with a more sophisticated parliamentary process, a more educated population infected with the imperialistic virus rampant on both sides of the Atlantic, and a huge business establishment, the proannexationists highlighted the business opportunities that were sure to come with the annexation of the Dominican Republic and the enlargement of the national empire. They also frequently found a sympathetic response from those policy-makers who desired an increased strategic U.S. military presence in the Caribbean. Unfortunately for proannexationists, the slower political apparatus allowed dissenters like Sumner to hamper the process of annexation.

Although the proannexationist forces differed in the two countries, many of their leaders were essentially "users." The most obvious, Cazneau and Fabens, used both the Dominican and United States governments to try to effect an annexation that they were sure would bring in a great deal of North American capital into the Dominican Republic. The Dominican people meant little to them and when the annexation scheme failed, they left the Dominican Republic instead of remaining and using their considerable ingenuity to help. Báez was among the worst presidents in Dominican history, accomplishing virtually nothing in his multiple terms. Clever in knowing that he had something that Grant wanted, he was also greatly skilled in using Cazneau and Fabens.

It is quite probable that Grant was aware of the shenanigans of Cazneau and Fabens and the kind of government Báez headed but was willing to tolerate them because the prize of territorial expansion in the Caribbean was worth the risk. A military man, he was not accustomed to communicating to the North American people just why the annexation of the Dominican Republic was so important, and so he thought that simply by using his operatives he could annex a foreign nation.[6]

It would be very satisfying to close this account on the note that, having been spared the fate of becoming a U.S. colony, the Dominican Republic emerged as an independent member of the family of nations. Unfortunately one is unable to make that observation. The Hartmont bonds on Báez's loan led to, among other things, a fiscal crisis in the Dominican Republic that paved the way for the "Dollar Diplomacy" of the United States.[7] Theodore Roosevelt, invoking his famous corollary to the Monroe Doctrine, took over the customs revenues of the Dominican Republic in 1905,[8] ostensibly to prevent European interference. Later, during the first North American occupation of 1916–24, North American economic influence continued virtually unabated, according to Wiarda and Kryzanek:

> The U.S. Occupation lasted eight years. These were years of economic growth, some modernization, and enforced political stability. The U.S. military fostered numerous public works projects (roads, telephones, port facilities), the foreign debt was decreased, educational facilities were built, and public health was improved. It is important to stress, however, that the United States was not so much an "enlightened civilizer" as a "pragmatic occupier." Its "modernization" of the Dominican Republic land titles system allowed American sugar firms to expand their holdings, the new roads were designed to facilitate the mobility of the occupation military forces, and the public works projects were paid for with *Dominican pesos.* [Emphasis added.][9]

As political analysts Jan Knippers Black and Howard Wiarda have suggested, the Dominican Republic is an "unsovereign state."[10] Nominally independent, its lack of a true autonomy has been demonstrated by the occupations by the United States in 1916–24 and in 1965. Although the United States has tried to downplay its autocratic role in unilaterally sending troops to the Dominican Republic in 1965 by pressuring the Organization of American States to send a token "peace-keeping force" to serve along with U.S. forces,[11] most observers of the Dominican scene then and now were aware that there was little that the Dominicans could have done to prevent the 1965 occupation, short of behaving in a manner consistent with U.S. interests.[12] In addition to the tremendous U.S. political and economic influence, there is a North American cultural incursion as well.

In the face of cultural, political, and economic domination by the United States over the Dominican Republic, students of Dominican history, as well as Dominicans themselves, might ask themselves if it would have been better if Charles Sumner, Carl Schurz, or less well-known people like Raymond Perry and J. Somers Smith had simply submitted to Grant and his agents and allowed the annexation of the Dominican Republic to be consummated. In the final analysis the answer will have to come from the actions of the Dominican people themselves. If they decide that material progress only, without national integrity, is the paramount concern, then it may well be that Sumner and his allies did the Dominicans a great disservice.

As most Dominicans know, the Puerto Ricans do not have any national sovereignty yet are living on a level that far exceeds Dominican present capabilities. Before the United States absorbs the Dominican Republic completely through its links with key industries, its military might, its arrangements with Dominican politicians, and its mesmerizing mass-media apparatus, Dominicans will have to decide just what nationhood means to them. If they do not, the narrative of the failed annexation of the Dominican Republic to the United States simply becomes a historical exercise, rather than the story of a heroic struggle to inspire future generations of Dominicans.

NOTES

1. Peguero and de los Santos, *Visión General*, 213–18.
2. Manuel Rodríguez Objío, *Gregorio Luperón*, 27–29. Luperón overcame his humble origins by sheer self-confidence.
3. Rodman, *Quisqueya*, 94.
4. McCulloch, *Men and Measures*, 234.
5. Interview with Dr. Pedro Ramón Vásquez y Vásquez, Director General, Archivo General de la Nación, in Santo Domingo, Dominican Republic, 8 January 1988. Dr. Vásquez y Vásquez observed that Sumner was certainly pivotal. He also indicated that the proximity of the Dominican Republic to the United States has deeply influenced its history.
6. It may be unfair to blame Grant for not being able to "galvanize support" for foreign adventure in the same way that Lincoln was able to harness the energies of the northern states. Tansill, *The Purchase*, chap. 1, has noted that in the aftermath of the Civil War the U.S. public was absorbed with pressing domestic problems. This preoccupation not only derailed Grant's annexation hopes but also stunted the accomplishment of the able and energetic William H. Seward.
7. Logan, *Haiti and the Dominican Republic*, 50, chap. 4.
8. Ibid., 54–55.
9. Wiarda and Kryzanek, *The Dominican Republic*, 33. The U.S. occupation of the Dominican Republic was not a humanitarian mission, which perhaps explains Wiarda's and Kryzanek's use of the word "pesos."
10. Ibid.; Black, *The Dominican Republic*.
11. Wiarda and Kryzanek, *The Dominican Republic*, 44–45.
12. Ibid. See also Abraham Lowenthal, "The United States and the Dominican Republic to 1965: Background to Intervention," *Caribbean Studies* 10 (July 1970): 30–55.

Appendix 1: Presidents of the Dominican Republic, 1844–1873

Name	Term of Office	Color
Pedro Santana	13 November 1844–4 August 1848	Mulatto
Manuel Jiménez	8 September 1848–29 May 1849	
Buenaventura Báez	24 September 1849–15 February 1853	Mulatto
Pedro Santana	15 February 1853–26 May 1856	Mulatto
Manuel de Regla Mota	26 May 1856–8 October 1856	
Buenaventura Báez	8 October 1856–7 July 1857	Mulatto
José Desiderio Valverde	7 July 1857–28 August 1858	
Provisional Government	28 August 1858–30 January 1859	
Pedro Santana	31 January 1859–18 March 1861	Mulatto
Spanish Occupation	18 March 1861–20 July 1865	
Pedro Antonio Pimentel	25 March 1865–13 August 1865	
José María Cabral	13 August 1865–8 December 1865	White
Buenaventura Báez	8 December 1865–28 May 1866	Mulatto
Provisional Government	28 May 1866–12 August 1866	
José María Cabral	22 August 1866–31 January 1868	White
Provisional Government	31 January 1868–2 May 1868	
Buenaventura Báez	2 May 1868–31 December 1873	Mulatto

While not covering the entire history of the Dominican Republic, the terms of the above political figures encompass dates that are most important to the annexation struggle described in this work. These dates are based on Bernardo Pichardo, *Resumen de Historia Patria* (Barcelona: Altés, 1930); Crassweller, *Trujillo;* Welles, *Naboth's Vineyard,* vol. 1, and Logan, *Haiti and the Dominican Republic.* The color is given when it is definitely known; when it is not shown, the president can be assumed to be white.

Appendix 2: Unperfected Treaties

DOMINICAN REPUBLIC

ANNEXATION

Secret bases for a definitive treaty signed at Santo Domingo September 4, 1869
Not subject to Senate action
Treaty file: Unperfected Treaty Series K-11
Printed text: none

Note: The Secret Bases were abandoned by mutual consent, and replaced by the treaty of December 29, 1869, unperfected (UTST) (Patterson). The original, in Spanish, could not be found; there is an English translation in the National Archives, General Records of the Department of State, Special Agents, vol. 24 (Orville E. Babcock, November 6, 1869); and a photocopy of the original, in Spanish with an English translation, in the treaty file. The present text is transcribed from the English translation in the National Archives.

SECRET BASES FOR A DEFINITIVE TREATY OF ANNEXATION.

TRANSLATION

The following bases, which shall serve for framing a definitive treaty between the United States and the Dominican Republic, have been reduced to writing and agreed upon by General Orville E. Babcock, aid de camp to His Excellency General Ulysses S. Grant, President of the United States of America and his Special Agent to the Dominican Republic, and Mr. Manuel María Gautier, Secretary of State of the Departments of the Interior and of Police, charged with the Foreign Relations of the said Dominican Republic.
I. His Excellency General Grant, President of the United States, promises,

Reprinted by permission from Christian L. Wiktor, editor and annotator. *Unperfected Treaties of the United States of America, 1776–1976*, 6 vols. (Dobbs Ferry, N. Y.: Oceana Publications, 1976), 2:347–49, 355–59, 361–63, 381–84.

privately to use all his influence in order that the idea of annexing the Dominican Republic to the United States may acquire such a degree of popularity among members of Congress, as will be necessary for its accomplishment; and he offers to make no communication to that Body on the subject, until he shall be certain that it will be approved by a majority.

The acceptance of annexation will oblige the United States to pay to the Dominican Republic the sum of one million five hundred thousand dollars in coin ($1,500,000) in order that that Republic may, as a State, pay its public debt, which is estimated at the said sum of a million five hundred thousand dollars in coin ($1,500,000); and the Dominican Republic, on its part, agrees to conform its Constitution to those of other States of the Union. In the event that the Dominican public debt should exceed one million five hundred thousand dollars in coin ($1,500,000) the excess shall be charged to the Dominican State.

II. In case the North American Congress shall reject the proposition for annexation, the Dominican government would accept as the price of the sale of Samaná, the two millions of dollars in coin ($2,000,000) which the same government of the United States offered it under the administration of President Johnson.

III. His Excellency President Grant assumes the obligation to remit, forthwith, to the Dominican Government, the sum of one hundred and fifty thousand dollars in coin ($150,000) a hundred thousand to be in cash and fifty thousand in arms, for the purpose of aiding in defraying the unavoidable expenses of the State. Credit shall be allowed for this amount, either on account of that which will be payable in the event of an acceptance of annexation, or of a preference for the acquisition of Samaná.

IV. In either case, the United States will guarantee the safety of the Country and of the government against every foreign aggression or machination, in order that the present Cabinet may carry into effect the obligation which it contracts, to obtain from the people, the expression of the national consent; which will necessarily have to be carried into effect within four months from the acceptance of the idea of annexation by President Grant.

V. It is understood by both parties, that if neither of the bases referred to shall be carried into effect, they shall be regarded as null and of no value or force, and that they shall, throughout all time, preserve their character of inviolable secrecy; but if one of the two extremes which they embrace shall be accepted (annexation of the Republic to the United States or the cession of Samaná) their tenor shall be obligatory for both parties and shall be embraced without change in the Definitive Treaty.

VI. In case the proposition relative to Samaná should alone be accepted by the United States, and the sum of one hundred thousand hard dollars should be remitted to this Capitol of San Domingo, as provided in Article 3, the Dominican government will abstain from receiving it until the Senate shall have approved the bargain, for which purpose it engages to submit that question and to solicit the said approval as soon as the said sum may arrive.

Done in duplicate, in good faith, in the City of St. Domingo, the fourth day of the month of September, in the year of our Lord one thousand eight hundred and sixty-nine.

Orville E. Babcock
Manuel María Gautier

DOMINICAN REPUBLIC

ANNEXATION

Treaty, with schedule of the property, signed at Santo Domingo November 29, 1869
Submitted to the Senate January 10, 1870
Ratification not advised by the Senate June 30, 1870
Ratified by the Dominican Republic prior to March 19, 1870
Treaty file: Unperfected Treaty Series T
Printed text: S. Conf. Ex. H, 41st Cong., 2d sess.; S. Ex. Doc. 17, 41st Cong., 3d sess., pp. 98-100 (serial no. 1440)

Note: The U.S. Senate rejected the treaty on June 30, 1870, by a vote of 28 to 28 (17 S. Ex. Journal 500–503; S. Journal 53(2) 379–380). See also the additional article of May 14, 1870, extending the time for the exchange of ratifications, unperfected (UTS I-7). Regarding the justification for the annexation, see President Ulysses S. Grant's second annual message to Congress of December 5, 1870 (7 Richardson 99–101); see also Moore, 1 Digest 278–280, 590–598. The original treaty with the schedule, in English and Spanish, is in the treaty file. The Senate print can be found in 69 Regular Confidential Documents 119, and subsequent volumes 70 to 73; with a copy in the Senate Records SEN 41B-B9. The present text is reprinted from a Senate print.

TREATY

CELEBRATED BETWEEN

THE U.S. OF AMERICA AND THE DOMINICAN REPUBLIC

FOR THE

Incorporation of the second with the first.

The people of the Dominican Republic having, through their government, expressed their desire to be incorporated into the United States as one of the Territories thereof, in order to provide more effectually for their security and prosperity; and the United States being desirous of meeting the wishes of the people and the government of that republic, the high contracting parties have determined to accomplish by treaty an object so important to their mutual and permanent welfare.

For this purpose the President of the United States has given full powers to Mr. Raymond H. Perry, United States commercial agent in the city of Santo Domingo, in the Dominican Republic, and the president of the Dominican Republic has given powers to Mr. Manuel María Gautier, secretary of state for foreign affairs of the said Dominican Republic; and the said plenipotentiaries, after having communicated to each other their respective full powers, found in good and due form, have agreed upon and concluded the following articles:

ARTICLE I.

The Dominican Republic, acting subject to the wishes of its people, to be expressed in the shortest possible time, renounces all rights of sovereignty as an independent sovereign nation, and cedes these rights to the United States to be incorporated by them as an integral portion of the Union, subject to the same constitutional provisions as their other Territories. It also cedes to the United States the absolute fee and property in all the custom-houses, fortifications, barracks, ports, harbors, navy and navy yards, magazines, arms, armaments, and accoutrements, archives, and public documents of the said Dominican Republic, of which a schedule is annexed to this treaty; public lands and other property not specified excepted.

ARTICLE II.

The citizens of the Dominican Republic shall be incorporated into the United States as citizens thereof, inhabiting one of its Territories, and shall be maintained and protected in the free enjoyment of their liberty and property as such citizens, and may be admitted into the Union as a State, upon such terms and conditions and at such time as Congress shall provide by law.

ARTICLE III.

The public lands and property belonging to the Dominican Republic, not herein specifically ceded to the United States, are pledged to the payment of all the public debt, liquidated or unliquidated, which shall remain after the payment provided for in this treaty.

ARTICLE IV.

The people of the Dominican Republic shall, in the shortest possible time, express in a manner conformable to their laws, their will concerning the cession herein provided for; and the United States shall, until such expression shall be had, protect the Dominican Republic against foreign interposition, in order that the national expression may be free.

ARTICLE V.

The United States shall pay to the Dominican Republic, for the property hereby ceded, the sum of one million five hundred thousand dollars in the gold coin of the United States, such payment not to be made until the Senate of the United States shall have given its advice and consent to the making of this treaty, and an appropriation for the payment shall have been made by Congress, and until delivery of all the property ceded shall be made to the persons authorized to receive the same.

ARTICLE VI.

The Dominican Republic engages to apply the amount so paid by the United States, through a commission to be appointed by the present actual Dominican government, toward the redemption of its public debt, in a manner conformable to the laws of said republic—this commission to be respected and protected by the United States while in the legal performance of its duties; and the said republic shall hold its public lands as a security for the payment of any part thereof, liquidated or unliquidated, which may remain unpaid after such application, and after the execution hereof to make no grants or concessions of lands or rights in lands and to contract no further debts until Congress shall assume jurisdiction over the Territory and officers shall be appointed to administer the affairs thereof. The United States are in no event to be liable for the payment of any part of such debt, or of the interest thereon, or of any obligation of the Dominican Republic.

ARTICLE VII.

Until provision shall be made by law for the government, as a Territory of the United States, of the domain hereby ceded, the laws of the Dominican Republic, which are not in conflict with the Constitution and laws of the United States, shall remain in force, and the executive and other public officers of the republic shall retain their offices until Congress shall enact laws for the government of the Territory, and until persons shall be appointed to office pursuant thereto.

ARTICLE VIII.

Immediately after the exchange of the ratifications of this treaty, the President of the United States shall appoint a commissioner to proceed to the Dominican Republic and receive the transfer of the domains and the property hereby ceded, subject to the foregoing provisions.

ARTICLE IX.

The present treaty shall be ratified by the contracting parties, it being understood that it must receive the constitutional advice and consent of the

Senate of the United States, before it can be ratified on the part of the United States, and the ratification shall be exchanged at Washington within four months from the date hereof, or sooner, if possible.

ARTICLE X.

In case of the rejection of this treaty the United States of America shall have the right to acquire the Peninsula and Bay of Samaná at any time prior to the expiration of a period of fifty years by paying to the Dominican Republic the sum of two million dollars in the gold coin of the United States.

ARTICLE XI.

It is understood that upon the ratification of this treaty the sum of one hundred and forty-seven thousand two hundred and twenty-nine dollars and ninety-one cents, paid by the United States to the Dominican Republic on account of the rent of Samaná, shall be deducted from the sum specified in Article V of this treaty.

In witness whereof, the respective plenipotentiaries have signed this treaty, and thereto affixed their respective seals.

Done in duplicate and good faith, in the English and Spanish languages, at the city of Santo Domingo, the twenty-ninth day of November, in the year of our Lord one thousand eight hundred and sixty-nine.

[SEAL.]   RAYMOND H. PERRY.
[SEAL.]   MANUEL MARÍA GAUTIER.

Schedule of the property mentioned in Article 1, to wit:

The stronghold of the city of Santo Domingo, which comprehends its walls, sixteen forts and small redoubts, two heavy batteries, various quarters, two powder magazines, the fortress called Homenage, and a park of artillery, with a full armament of cannon and mortars, iron and brass; shells, grenades, grape, muskets, and various other utensils and instruments indispensable to a fortified place.

The Castle of San Jeronimo.

The Castle of Haina, on the river of that name.

The Fort San Luis, at Santiago de los Caballeros.

The Castle of San Felipe, at Puerto Plata.

The Fort of San Francisco, at Monte Christi.

The Fort of Santa Barbara, at Samaná.

The Fort of Los Cacaos, at the same place.

The Custom-house at Santo Domingo and its dependencies.

The Custom-house at Samaná, built of timber.

The ports of Santo Domingo, Macorís, Azua, Samaná, Puerto Plata, and Monte Christi, which are those which are licensed for commerce with foreigners.

There are, moreover, an infinity of ports, bays, and coves which could be applied to similar use, especially Barahona, Puerto Viejo de Azua, La Caldera, La Romana, Chavón, Matanzas, and Manzanillo. Various other points intended for fortifications, military stations, and which either have been removed or not yet been erected.

Witness the hands of the said plenipotentiaries, at the city of Santo Domingo, the 29th day of November, A.D. 1869.

RAYMOND H. PERRY.

MANUEL MARÍA GAUTIER.

DOMINICAN REPUBLIC

LEASE OF THE BAY AND PENINSULA OF SAMANÁ

Convention signed at Santo Domingo November 29, 1869
Submitted to the Senate January 10, 1870
No final action by the Senate
Treaty file: Unperfected Treaty Series G-7
Printed text: S. Conf. Ex. G, 41st Cong., 2d sess.; S. Ex. Doc. 17, 41st Cong., 3d sess., pp. 101–102 (serial no. 1440)

Note: The U.S. Senate took no final action (Patterson). See also the additional article of July 7, 1870, extending the time for the exchange of ratifications, unperfected (UTS U). For more information see Moore, 1 Digest 598–600. The original convention, in English and Spanish, was transmitted to the National Archives in compliance with Senate Resolution 268, 72d Cong., 1st sess., of July 9, 1932 (S. Journal 72 (1) 691-692; 75 Cong. Record 14961), and is now in the treaty file. The Senate print can be found in 69 Regular Confidential Documents 105, and subsequent volumes 70 to 73; with a copy in the Senate Records SEN 41B-B8. The present text is reprinted from a Senate print.

CONVENTION

CELEBRATED BETWEEN

THE UNITED STATES OF AMERICA AND THE DOMINICAN REPUBLIC FOR A LEASE OF THE BAY AND PENINSULA OF SAMANÁ.

For this purpose the President of the United States has invested with full powers Mr. Raymond H. Perry, commercial agent of the United States to the Dominican Republic, and the President of the Dominican Republic has invested with full powers Mr. Manuel María Gautier, secretary of state of the Dominican Republic, who, after exchanging their said full powers, found in good and due form, have agreed upon, concluded, and signed the following articles:

ARTICLE I.

The Dominican Republic grants immediate possession and occupation, in the form of a lease, to the United States of America, all the territory comprised in the peninsula and bay of Samaná, extending from Cape Samaná or Rezón to the R. Grand Estero, which begins at the mouth of the said Grand Estero on the north, and terminates at the mouth of the Trujillo, at the western end of the bay of Samaná, as appears on the map of the island of Santo Domingo, executed by Sir Robert H. Schomburgk, and published in 1858 by order of his excellency President Buenaventura Báez.

The United States shall possess and occupy the above-described territory during a period of 50 years from this date, and the Dominican Republic cedes by this net to the United States the eminent domain of said territory during the above described term of occupation.

It is understood that the Dominican Republic does not cede its right of free navigation of the waters of said bay.

ARTICLE II.

During the above-named term of occupation of the said territory the United States shall pay, as an annual rent, to the Dominican Republic, on the first day of January of each year, in Washington, D.C., or in the city of New York, the sum of one hundred and fifty thousand dollars in gold coin of the United States. The Dominican Republic hereby acknowledges to have received the sum of one hundred and forty-seven thousand two hundred and twenty-nine dollars and ninety-one cents on account of the first payment under this convention.

ARTICLE III.

In case the United States shall establish a naval and military station, or either, on any part of the tract hereinabove described, the Dominican Republic shall, on demand of the chief officer in command thereof, arrest and surrender to the United States all deserters from the army or navy of the United States found within the said territory of the Dominican Republic, but the expense of such arrest and surrender shall be borne by the United States.

ARTICLE IV.

This convention shall be ratified by both parties, it being understood that it cannot be ratified by the United States until it has received the advice and consent of the Senate of the United States; and the ratification shall take place at Washington, D.C., as soon as possible within four months from the date hereof.

The United States shall protect the Dominican Republic against foreign intervention during the time agreed upon for exchange of the above ratification.

Done in duplicate and good faith in the English and Spanish languages, in the city of Santo Domingo, the twenty-ninth day of the month of November, in the year of our Lord one thousand eight hundred and sixty-nine.

[SEAL.]   RAYMOND H. PERRY.
[SEAL.]   MANUEL MARÍA GAUTIER.

DOMINICAN REPUBLIC

ANNEXATION.
EXTENSION OF TIME

Additional article signed at Washington May 14, 1870
Submitted to the Senate May 31, 1870
Treaty file: Unperfected Treaty Series I-7
Printed text: S. Conf. Ex. S, 41st Cong., 2d sess.

Note: With the rejection by the U.S. Senate on June 30, 1870, of the treaty of November 29, 1869, unperfected (UTS T), this additional article became obsolete (see also List of Treaties (1789–1931), p. 17, note H; and List of Treaties (1789–1934), p. 74, no. 248). The original additional article, in English, was transmitted to the National Archives in compliance with Senate Resolution 268, 72d Cong., 1st sess., of July 9, 1932 (S. Journal 72 (1) 691-692; 75 Cong. Record 14961),and is now in the treaty file. The Senate print can be found in 69 Regular Confidential Documents 171, and subsequent volumes 70 to 73; with a copy in the Senate Records SEN 41B-B10. The present text is reprinted from a Senate print.

ADDITIONAL ARTICLE TO THE TREATY BETWEEN THE UNITED STATES AND THE DOMINICAN REPUBLIC OF THE TWENTY-NINTH OF NOVEMBER, EIGHTEEN HUNDRED AND SIXTY-NINE, FOR THE ANNEXATION OF THAT REPUBLIC TO THE UNITED STATES.

Whereas, pursuant to the IXth article of the treaty between the United States and the Dominican Republic, of the twenty-ninth day of November, eighteen hundred and sixty-nine, for the annexation of that republic to the United States, it was stipulated that the ratifications of that instrument should be exchanged within four months from its date, or sooner, if possible; and whereas the said time has expired, but the parties being still desirous that the said treaty should be carried into full effect, have determined to extend the time for the exchange of the ratifications aforesaid: For this purpose the President of the United States has conferred full powers on Hamilton Fish, Secretary of State, and the President of the Dominican Republic has conferred like powers on Joseph Warren Fabens; and the said plenipotentiaries having exchanged their full powers, which were found to be in due form, have agreed upon the following

ADDITIONAL ARTICLE.

The time for exchanging the ratifications of the treaty between the United States and the Dominican Republic of the 29th of November, 1869, is hereby extended to the first day of July next.

In witness whereof the respective plenipotentiaries have signed the present article in duplicate, and have affixed thereto their seals.

Done at Washington the 14th day of May, 1870.

[L.S.]   HAMILTON FISH.
[L.S.]   JOSEPH WARREN FABENS.

DOMINICAN REPUBLIC

LEASE OF THE BAY AND PENINSULA OF SAMANÁ. EXTENSION OF TIME

Additional article signed at Washington July 7, 1870
Not submitted to the Senate
Treaty file: Unperfected Treaty Series U
Printed text: none

Note: The additional article was submitted to the Senate, with a copy of the treaty, by President Ulysses S. Grant on July 8, 1870 (see List of Treaties (1789–1934), p. 74, note 249; and List of Treaties (1789–1931), pp. 16–17, note G). The submission is not mentioned in the S. Ex. Journal or in Richardson. The original Presidential message of July 8, 1870, is in the treaty file and not in the Senate Records (see Carroll). It would seem that the article was not received by the Senate. See also convention of November 29, 1869, unperfected (UTS G-7). The original additional article, in English, together with a printer's copy, is in the treaty file. The present text is transcribed from the original in the treaty file.

ADDITIONAL ARTICLE OF THE CONVENTION BETWEEN THE UNITED STATES AND THE DOMINICAN REPUBLIC OF THE TWENTY-NINTH OF NOVEMBER, EIGHTEEN HUNDRED AND SIXTY-NINE, FOR A LEASE OF THE BAY AND PENINSULA OF SAMANÁ.

Whereas, pursuant to the IV Article of the Convention between the United States and the Dominican Republic of the twenty-ninth day of

November, eighteen hundred and sixty-nine, for a lease of the Bay and Peninsula of Samaná, it was stipulated that the ratification of that instrument should take place at Washington as soon as possible within four months from its date.

And whereas the said time has expired, but the parties being still desirous that the said Convention should be carried into full effect, have determined to extend the time for the ratification aforesaid. For this purpose the President of the United States has conferred full powers on Hamilton Fish, Secretary of State, and the President of the Dominican Republic has conferred like powers on Joseph Warren Fabens;

And the said Plenipotentiaries having exchanged their full powers, which were found to be in due form have agreed upon the following.

Additional Article.

The time for ratifying at Washington the Convention between the United States and the Dominican Republic of the 29th of November 1869, for a lease of the Bay and Peninsula of Samaná is hereby extended to the first day of July next.

In witness whereof, the respective plenipotentiaries have signed the present article in duplicate and have affixed thereto their seals.

Done at Washington the seventh day of July, 1870.

[Seal] Hamilton Fish
[Seal] Joseph Warren Fabens

Appendix 3: Important Dates and Times (to 1871)

12 October 1492: Christopher Columbus establishes first permanent European presence in the New World.

February 1502: Nicolás de Ovando starts Santo Domingo's first real development as a Spanish colony.

20 September 1697: The Treaty of Ryswick officially grants the French possession over the western third of Hispaniola.

22 August 1791: Black slaves revolt in the French part of Hispaniola, Saint-Domingue, starting a process that resulted in the establishment of Haiti.

22 July 1795: The Treaty of Basel cedes the entire Spanish part of Hispaniola to the French.

26–27 January 1801: Toussaint L'Ouverture takes possession of Santo Domingo City.

1 January 1804: Jean Jacques Dessalines proclaims the independence of Haiti.

October–November 1808: Juan Sánchez Ramírez leads a creole revolt against French presence in Santo Domingo, leading to the establishment of *España Boba*.

30 November 1821: José Núñez de Cáceres proclaims the independence of "Spanish Haiti."

9 February 1822: The Haitian occupation of Santo Domingo begins.

July 1825: Start of Haitian president Jean-Pierre Boyer's indemnities to France for its recognition of Haiti.

16 July 1838: La Trinitaria movement founded by Dominican creole Juan Pablo Duarte.

15 September 1843: Release of a paper directed to the French government specifying terms for French control of Santo Domingo.

27 February 1844: Declaration of independence of Santo Domingo from Haiti. Founding of the Dominican Republic.

6 January 1845: Dominican envoy José M. Caminero received by U.S. Secretary of State John C. Calhoun, arousing U.S. interest in the Dominican Republic.

May 1846: U.S. naval lieutenant David D. Porter travels to various parts of the Dominican Republic. Reports the utility of Samaná as a naval base site.

3 October 1849: Dominican Government of Buenaventura Báez inquires officially of the U.S. commercial agent about annexation by the United States.

24 July 1851: France and Britain intercede against Haitian aggression toward the Dominican Republic.

18 October 1854: The Ostend Manifesto, signed by U.S. ministers Pierre Soulé, James Buchanan, and John Mason, expresses U.S. aggressive designs in the Caribbean.

23 November–5 December 1854: Final defeat of a commercial treaty between the United States and the Dominican Republic that would have given the United States a foothold in Samaná. This was the culmination of a long fight by the British and the French against the treaty.

18 March 1861: Restoration of Spanish sovereignty in Santo Domingo.

20 July 1865: Departure of the last of the Spanish troops.

6 September 1865: Jane McManus (Cora Montgomery) Cazneau writes a letter to U.S. Secretary of the Interior James Harlan that results in the arousal of U.S. Secretary of State William H. Seward's interest in Dominican territory as a naval base site.

9 December 1868: U.S. President Andrew Johnson officially puts on record the interest of a U.S. chief executive in the annexation of the Dominican Republic to the United States.

12 January 1869: General Nathaniel P. Banks, chairman of the U.S. House Committee on Foreign Affairs, sponsors a resolution that authorizes the president to extend U.S. protection to the governments of Haiti and the Dominican Republic. It is defeated.

1 February 1869: U.S. Congressman Godlove Orth introduces a resolution calling for the annexation of the territory of "San Domingo." This, too, is defeated, but by a narrower margin.

1 May 1869: Date of the Hartmont loan to the Dominican Republic. The terms of this loan were so oppressive that the measures future Dominican governments would have to take to meet payment played a large part in the establishment of U.S. "Dollar Diplomacy" in the Dominican Republic.

1 June 1869: Gregorio Luperón gives an inspired speech in Puerto Plata on the dangers of annexation and thereafter steps up his harassing naval activities, which resulted in U.S. naval interference.

10 July 1869: U.S. Commander E. K. Owen is instructed to sail for Dominican waters and search out Luperón's naval vessel, *The Telégrafo.*

4 September 1869: A treaty outline, signed in the Dominican Republic by U.S. envoy Orville Babcock and Dominican minister Manuel Gautier, calls for U.S. President Grant to use all his influence to see that an annexation treaty is passed.

29 November 1869: Signing of the dual treaty for annexation of the Dominican Republic and the lease of Samaná. This treaty was to be ratified by the United States within four months of this signing.

4 December 1969: U.S. Generals Babcock, Sackett, and Ingalls formally take possession of Samaná in accordance with the terms of the 29 November treaty.

January 1870: Emergence of U.S. Senator Charles Sumner as Grant's formidable opponent in the annexation fight.

January 1870: Capture of Haitian President Sylvain Salnave (an ally of Báez) by Dominican General José María Cabral. Later he was turned over to Haitian revolutionary leader Nissage-Saget, who had him shot.

16–20 February 1870: Plebiscite to vote on annexation is held in the Dominican Republic. The vote is 16,000 to 11 for annexation.

29 March 1870: Annexation treaty expires by limitation, in spite of Grant's efforts.

14 May 1870: U.S. Secretary of State Hamilton Fish signs an article calling for an extension of the time needed for the exchange of ratifications of the annexation treaty.

29 June 1870: The vote taken in the U.S. Senate on the treaty of annexation ends in a tie—short of the two-thirds favorable vote needed for ratification.

7 July 1870: Grant arranges for Joseph W. Fabens and Hamilton Fish to sign an article that would extend the time needed for the exchange of ratifications to 1 July 1871. Through an oversight this article was never submitted to the Senate.

5 December 1870: Grant sends to Congress a message recommending a joint resolution authorizing him to appoint a joint commission to negotiate a treaty with Dominican authorities for the island's acquisition by the United States.

5 April 1871: Grant defers the question of the Dominican annexation to the American people, signifying his recognition of defeat by Congress.

Appendix 4: The Many Faces of Hispaniola, 1492 to 1989

1492–1697

1697–1795

1795–1804

1804–9

1809–21

*1821–22

1822–44

1844–61

1861–65

1865–1915

1915–16

†1916–24

1924–34

‡1934–1989

133

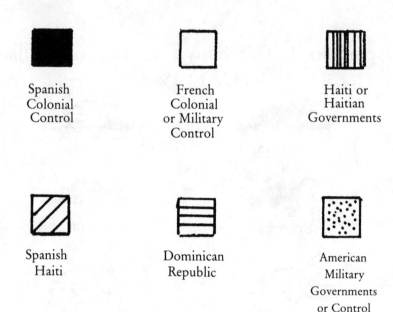

Spanish
Colonial
Control

French
Colonial
or Military
Control

Haiti or
Haitian
Governments

Spanish
Haiti

Dominican
Republic

American
Military
Governments
or Control

*The period given is misleading, since the nation of "Spanish Haiti" was in existence for only a matter of weeks; moreover, most historians view the real start of Dominican independence as taking place in 1844.

†Even during the U.S. military presence in Haiti, Haiti had official (puppet) presidents, unlike the Dominican Republic when it was occupied from 1916 to 1922. The last two years of U.S. occupation of the Dominican Republic (1922–24) were marked by the appearance of a Dominican "Provisional President."

‡Excepting the period in which U.S. armed forces, or U.S.-dominated "peacekeeping forces," occupied the Dominican Republic from 28 April 1965 to 21 September 1966.

Bibliography

Primary Sources

MANUSCRIPT COLLECTIONS

Boston. Public Library. Department of Rare Books and Manuscripts. Benjamin Hunt, "Newspaper History of the Annexation of the Dominican Republic from July 1869 to July 1870." 5 vols.

Cambridge. Harvard University, Houghton Library. Manuscript Department. Charles Sumner Papers.

Durham, North Carolina. Duke University, Perkins Library. Manuscript Division. David D. Porter Papers.

Rochester, New York. University of Rochester, Rush Rhees Library. Department of Rare Books and Manuscripts. William H. Seward Papers.

Santo Domingo, Dominican Republic. Archivo General de la Nación. Secciones de Relaciones Exteriores, 1871.

Washington, D.C. Library of Congress. Manuscript Division.

Nathaniel P. Banks Papers

Benjamin F. Butler Papers

Diary of Hamilton Fish

Ulysses S. Grant Papers

DeBenneville R. Keim Papers

Carl Schurz Papers

Elihu Washburne Papers

Washington, D.C. Department of State. Manuscript Division.

Instructions to Consuls

Reports of the Secretary of State to the President and Congress

NEWSPAPERS

Boletín Oficial (Santo Domingo), 1870
Boston Morning Journal (Boston), 1877
New York Herald (New York), 1869–70
New York Times (New York), 1870
New York Tribune (New York), 1871
New York World (New York), 1870

PUBLIC DOCUMENTS

London England, Public Record Office, Foreign Office Papers F.O. 5/1193 No. 284, 264.

Washington, D.C.

Communications Received by the Department of State from Special Agents of the Department of State, 1794–1906, 1852–61, M 37/Roll 9

Despatches from Special Agents to the Department of State, 1847–50, M 37/Roll 15

Despatches from United States Consuls in Cap Haitien, 1797–1906, 1858–69, M 9/Roll 9

Despatches from United States Consuls in Santo Domingo, 1837–1906, T 56/Roll 4, T 56/Roll 5; 1861–71, T 56/Roll 6; 1874–77, T 56/Roll 8

Diplomatic Instructions of the Department of State, 1801–1906, 1852–86, M 77/Roll 153

Domestic Letters of the Department of State, 1784–1906, 1868–69, M 40/Roll 65

Notes from the Legations of the Dominican Republic in the United States to the Department of State, 1844–1906, 1869–71, T 801/Roll 1

Pan American General Secretary, Organization of American States, Department of Public Instruction, Pan American Union, Washington, D.C. 21 volumes. *The Dominican Republic* (vol. 8), 1964.

U.S. Congress. *Congressional Globe*, 46 vols., 1834–73, 1869–71, 40 Cong. 3 sess., 12 January 1869, 13 January 1869, 1 February 1869; 41 Cong. 3 sess., 9 December 1870; 12 December 1870, 21 December 1870; 27 March 1871.

U.S. Congress. Senate.

Journal of the Executive Proceedings of the Senate of the United States, 5 March 1869–3 March 1871, vol. 17, Washington: Govt. Printing Office, 1901

Report of the U.S. Select Committee on the Memorial of Davis Hatch, 1870

Senate Executive Documents, 1869–71, 41 Cong. 3 Sess. No. 17, 16 January 1871; 41 Cong. 3 Sess. No. 34, 7 February 1871; 42 Cong. 1 Sess. No. 9, 5 April 1871

SECONDARY SOURCES

ARTICLES AND PAPERS

Bancroft, Frederic, and William Dunning. "A Sketch of Carl Schurz' Political Career." In *Reminiscences,* edited by Carl Schurz. 3 vols. New York: McClure Co., 1908.

Baur, John Edward. "Mulatto Machiavelli: Jean-Pierre Boyer and the Haiti of His Day." *Journal of Negro History* 32 (July 1947): 307–53.

Bloomfield, Richard J. Introduction to *Puerto Rico: The Search for a National Policy,* edited by Richard J. Bloomfield. Boulder, Colo.: Westview Press, 1985.

Cox, Jacob. D. "How Judge Hoar Ceased to be Attorney General." *Atlantic Monthly* 76 (August 1895): 162–73.

Dunning, W. A. "Paying for Alaska." *Political Science Quarterly* 27 (1912): 385–98.

Fabens, Joseph W. "The Uses of the Camel: Considered with a View to His Introduction into Our Western States and Territories." Paper presented at the annual meeting of the American Geographical and Statistical Society, New York, 2 March 1865.

Hauch, Charles C. "Fuentes en los Estados Unidos Relativas al Proyecto de Anexión de la República Dominicana, 1869–1871." *Boletín del Archivo General de la Nación* 4 (August 1941): 183–87.

Hoetink, H. "Materiales para el Estudio de la República Dominicana en la Segunda Mitad del Siglo XIX." *Caribbean Studies* 7 (1967): 3–34.

Lacerte, Robert K. "Xenophobia and Economic Decline: The Haitian Case, 1820–1843." *Americas* 37 (April 1981): 499–515.

León Portilla, Miguel. "The Grief of the Conquered: 'Broken Spears Lie in the Roads.'" In *Latin America: A Historical Reader,* edited by Lewis Hanke. Boston: Little Brown, 1974.

Lowenthal, Abraham. "The United States and the Dominican Republic to 1965: Background to Intervention." *Caribbean Studies* 10 (July 1970): 30–55.

"Mensaje a la Comisión de Investigación de E.U.A. en Santo Domingo, Febrero 3 de 1871." *Boletín del Archivo General de la Nación* 23 (1960): 101–8.

Morales Carrión, Arturo. "The Need for a New Encounter." In *Puerto Rico: The Search for a National Policy,* edited by Richard J. Bloomfield. Boulder, Colo.: Westview Press, 1985.

Nelson, William Javier. "The Crisis of Liberalism in the Dominican Republic, 1865–1882." *Revista de Historia de América* 104 (July–December 1987): 19–29.

———. "Debt of Gratitude? British and French Circumvention of the Treaty of 1854 between the Dominican Republic and the United States." *Journal of Caribbean Studies* 6 (Autumn 1988): 275–85.

———. "The Haitian Political Situation and Its Effect on the Dominican Republic." *Americas* 45 (1988): 227–35.

———. "Notes on Dominican Race Relations." Paper presented at the annual meeting of the Southeast Conference on Latin American Studies, Clemson, S.C., April 1986.

"Proclama a los Dominicanos, Curaçao 18 de Marzo de 1870." *Boletín del Archivo General de la Nación* 23 (November–December 1960): 8–9.

Segal, Aaron. "The Caribbean Exodus." Paper presented at the annual meeting of the Southeast Conference on Latin American Studies, Clemson, South Carolina, April 1986.

Smith, Theodore C. "Expansion after the Civil War, 1865–1871." *Political Science Quarterly* 16 (September 1901): 412–36.

Steward, Julian H., Robert A. Manners, Erik R. Wolf, Elena Padilla Seda, Sidney W. Mintz, and Raymond Scheele. "National Patterns during the American Period, 1898–1948." In *The People of Puerto Rico,* edited by Julian H. Seward. Urbana: University of Illinois Press, 1969.

Tansill, Charles Callan. "War Powers of the President." *Political Science Quarterly* 45 (March 1930): 1–55.

Van Alstyne, R. W. "Anglo-American Relations, 1853–1857." *American Historical Review* 42 (1937): 491–500.

Winch, Julie. "American Free Blacks and Emigration to Haiti." *C.I.S.C.L.A. Working Paper Series (Documentos de Trabajo)* no. 33 (August 1988): 1–22.

———. "Jean-Pierre Boyer and The American Immigration to Haiti." Paper presented at the annual meeting of the Association of Caribbean Studies, Bahía, Brazil, July 1986.

BOOKS

Adams, Charles F. *Lee at Appomattox and Other Papers*, 2d. ed. Boston: Houghton Mifflin and Co., 1902.

Allen, H. C. *Great Britain and the United States: A History of Anglo-American Relations*. New York: St. Martin's Press, 1955.

Ammen, David. *The Old Navy and the New*. Philadelphia: J. B. Lippincott Co., 1891.

Arango, E. Ramón. *The Spanish Political System: Franco's Legacy*. Boulder, Colo.: Westview Press, 1978.

Archambault, Pedro M. *Historia de la Restauración*. 2d ed. Santo Domingo: Ediciones de Taller, 1973.

Badeau, Adam. *Grant in Peace*. Hartford, Conn.: S. S. Scranton & Co., 1887.

Bailey, Helen Miller, and Abraham Nasatir. *Latin America: The Development of Its Civilization*. Englewood Cliffs, N.J.: Prentice-Hall, 1973.

Baker, George E. *The Works of William H. Seward*. 5 vols. New York: Redfield. Boston: Houghton Mifflin and Co., 1853–84.

Balaguer, Joaquín. *Colón: Precursor Literario*. Mexico City: Fuentes Impresores, 1974.

Balcácer, Juan Daniel. *Pedro Santana: Historia Política de un Déspota*. Santo Domingo: Editora Taller, 1974.

Bell, Ian. *The Dominican Republic*. Boulder, Colo.: Westview Press, 1981.

Bennett, Lerone. *Before the Mayflower*. Chicago: Johnson Publishing Co., 1962.

Betances de Pujadas, Estrella. *Origen y Proyecciones del Protectoralismo Dominicano*. Santo Domingo: Editora Alfa y Omega, 1979.

Bigelow, John. *Retrospections of an Active Life*. 4 vols. Garden City, N.Y.: Doubleday, Page and Co., 1913.

Black, Jan Knippers. *The Dominican Republic: Politics and Development in an Unsovereign State*. Boston: Allen and Unwin, 1986.

Blaine, James G. *Twenty Years of Congress*. 2 vols. Norwich, Conn.: Henry Bill Publishing Co., 1886.

Boin, Jacqueline, and José Serulle Ramía. *El Proceso de Desarrollo del Capitalismo en la República Dominicana*. Santo Domingo: Ediciones Gramil, 1980.

Bosch, Juan. *The Unfinished Experiment: Democracy in the Dominican Republic*. New York: Frederick A. Praeger, 1964.

Brown, Charles. *Agents of Manifest Destiny*. Chapel Hill: University of North Carolina Press, 1980.

Carr, Ramona. *Puerto Rico: A Colonial Experiment*. New York: New York University Press, 1984.

Carr, Raymond. *Spain, 1808–1975*. 2d ed. Oxford: Clarendon Press, 1982.

Cazneau, Jane McManus. *Our Winter Eden: Pen Pictures of the Tropics*. New York: The Authors Publishing Co., 1878.

Cazneau, William L. *To the American Press: The Dominican Negotiations*. Santo Domingo: García Hermanos, 1870.

Cestero, Tulio M. *Estados Unidos y las Antillas*. Madrid: Compañía Ibero-Americana de Publicaciones, 1931.

Clarke, H. Butler. *Modern Spain, 1815–1898*. New York: A.M.S. Press, 1969.

Cole, Cornelius. *Memoirs*. New York: McLoughlin Brothers, 1908.

Crassweller, Robert D. *Trujillo: The Life and Times of a Caribbean Dictator*. New York: MacMillan Co., 1966.

Craven, Avery. *The United States: Experiment in Democracy*. Boston: Ginn and Co., 1962.

Current, Richard N., T. Harry Williams, Frank Freidel, and W. Elliot Brownlee. *The Essentials of American History*, 2d ed. New York: Alfred A. Knopf, 1976.

D'Alaux, Gustave. *L'Emperor Soulouque et son Empire*. Paris: Michel Lévy Fréres, 1856.

del Monte y Tejada, Antonio. *Historia de Santo Domingo*. 3d ed. 6 vols. Santo Domingo: Biblioteca Dominicana, 1952.

Fagg, John Edwin. *Cuba, Haiti and the Dominican Republic*. Englewood Cliffs, N.J.: Prentice-Hall, 1956.

Franco Pichardo, Franklin J. *Los Negros, los Mulatos y la Nación Dominicana*. Santo Domingo: Editora Nacional, 1970.

———. *La República Dominicana: Clases, Crisis y Comandos*. Havana: Casa de las Américas, 1966.

García, José Gabriel. *Examen Critico del Informe de los Comisionados de Santo Domingo Dedicado al Pueblo de los Estados Unidos*. Caracas: A.L.S. Muller, C. J. & A. W. Newman, 1871.

———. *Historia Moderna de la República Dominicana*. In *Compendio de la Historia de Santo Domingo*. 3d ed. 4 vols. Santo Domingo: Imprenta de García Hermanos, 1906.

Garrido, Víctor. *Política de Francia en Santo Domingo, 1844–1846*. Santo Domingo: Editora del Caribe, 1962.

Gimbernard, Jacinto. *Historia de Santo Domingo*. 7th ed. Madrid: M. Fernández y Cía, S.A., 1978.

Goslinga, C.Ch. *Curaçao and Guzmán Blanco: A Case Study of Small Power Politics in the Caribbean*. The Hague: Martinus Nijhoff, 1975.

Grant, Jesse R. *In the Days of My Father, General Grant*. New York: Harper Brothers Publishers, 1925.

Harris, Marvin, *Patterns of Race in the Americas*. New York: Walker, 1964.

Havistock, Nathan, and John P. Hoover. *The Dominican Republic*. New York: Sterling Publishing Co., 1979.

Hazard, Samuel. *Santo Domingo, Past and Present*. London: Sampson Low, Marston, Low and Searle, 1873.

Heinl, Robert D., and Nancy Gordon Heinl. *Written in Blood: The Story of the Haitian People*. Boston: Houghton Mifflin Co., 1978.

Henríquez Ureña, Max. *Los Yanquis en Santo Domingo*. Madrid: Impresora de J. Pueyo, 1929.

Hoetink, H. *The Dominican People, 1850–1900: Notes for a Historical Sociology*. Baltimore: Johns Hopkins University Press, 1982.

Holmes, Oliver Wendell. *John Lothrop Motley*. Boston: Houghton Osgood & Co., 1879.

Holt, W. Stull. *Treaties Defeated by the Senate.* Gloucester, Mass.: Peter B. Smith, 1964.

Howe, Samuel G. *Letters on the Proposed Annexation of Santo Domingo.* Boston: Wright and Potter, 1871.

Hume, Martin A. S. *Modern Spain, 1788–1898.* New York: G. P. Putnam's Sons, 1909.

James, C. L. R. *The Black Jacobins: Toussaint L'Ouverture and the San Domingo Revolution.* New York: Dial Press, 1938.

James, Preston E. *Introduction to Latin America.* Indianapolis: Odyssey Press, 1964.

Jennings, Lawrence C. *France and Europe in 1848: A Study of French Foreign Affairs in Time of Crisis.* London: Oxford University Press, 1973.

Jiménez Grullón, Juan Isidro. *La República Dominicana: Una Ficción.* Mérida, Venezuela: Talleres Gráficos Universitarios, 1965.

Keim, DeBenneville R. *Santo Domingo.* Philadelphia: Claxton, Remsen & Haffelfinger, 1870.

Knight, Melvin. *The Americans in Santo Domingo.* New York: Vanguard Press, 1928. Reprinted as *Los Americanos en Santo Domingo: Episodios de Imperialismo Americano.* Santo Domingo: Editora de Santo Domingo, 1980.

Latimer, Elizabeth Wormeley. *Spain in the Nineteenth Century.* Chicago: A. C. McClurg and Co., 1898.

Lebrón Saviñón, Mariano. *Historia de la Cultura Dominicana.* 2 vols. Santo Domingo: Universidad Nacional Pedro Henríquez Ureña, 1981.

Leger, Jacques Nicolás. *Haiti: Her History and Her Detractors.* Westport, Conn.: Negro Universities Press, 1907.

Logan, Rayford. *Haiti and the Dominican Republic.* New York: Oxford University Press, 1968.

López Morillo, Adriano. *Memorias de la Segunda Reincorporación de Santo Domingo a España.* 3 vols. Santo Domingo: Editora Corripio, C. por A., 1983.

Luperón, Gregorio. *Notas Autobiográficas y Apuntes Historicos.* Reprint. Santo Domingo. Editora de Santo Domingo, 1974.

McCulloch, Hugh. *Men and Measures of Half a Century.* New York: Charles Scribners Sons, 1888.

Manning, William Ray, comp. *Diplomatic Correspondence of the United States: Inter-American Affairs, 1831–1860.* 12 vols. Washington, D.C.: Carnegie Endowment for International Peace, 1932–39.

Matloff, Maurice, ed. *American Military History.* Washington, D.C.: Office of Chief of Military History, 1969.

Merk, Frederick. *Manifest Destiny and Mission in American History.* New York: Alfred A. Knopf, 1963.

Monclús, Miguel Angel. *El Caudillismo en la República Dominicana.* 3d ed. Santo Domingo: Editora del Caribe, 1962.

Montague, Ludwell Lee. *Haiti and the United States, 1714–1938.* Durham, N.C.: Duke University Press, 1940.

Moreau de Saint-Méry, Médéric-Louis-Elie. *Description Topographique, Physique, Civile, Politique et Historique de la Partie Française de L'Isle de Saint-Domingue.* 3 vols. Paris: Société de L'Histoire des Colonies Françaises, 1958.

———. *A Topographical and Political Description of the Spanish Part of Santo*

Domingo. Translated by William Cobbett. 2 vols. Philadelphia: Author, printer and bookseller, 1796.

Moya Pons, Frank. *Historia Colonial de Santo Domingo*. Santiago: Universidad Católica Madre y Maestra, 1974.

———. *Manual de Historia Dominicana*. 7th ed. Santiago: Universidad Católica Madre y Maestra, 1983.

Nelson, William Javier. *Racial Definition Handbook*. Minneapolis, Minn.: Burgess Publishing Co., 1982.

Nevins, Allan. *Hamilton Fish*. New York: Dodd Mead and Co., 1936.

Oberholtzer, Ellis P. *A History of the United States since the Civil War*. 5 vols. New York: MacMillan & Co., 1922.

Osorio Lizarazo, J. A. *La Isla Iluminada*. Santo Domingo: Editora del Caribe, 1953.

Paolino, Ernest N. *The Foundations of the American Empire: William Henry Seward and U.S. Foreign Policy*. Ithaca, N.Y.: Cornell University Press, 1973.

Parton, James. *Danish Islands: Are We Bound in Honor to Pay for Them?* Boston: Fields, Osgood and Co., 1869.

Pattee, Ricardo. *La República Dominicana*. Madrid: Ediciones Cultura Hispana, 1967.

Peguero, Valentina, and Danilo de los Santos. *Visión General de la Historia Dominicana*. Santo Domingo: Editora Taller, 1981.

Peña Batlle, Manuel A. *La Isla de la Tortuga*. Santo Domingo: Ediciones de Cultura Hispánica, 1971.

Pérez y Pérez, Carlos Federico. *Historia Diplomática de Santo Domingo, 1492–1861*. Santo Domingo: Universidad Nacional Pedro Henríquez Ureña, 1973.

———. *El Pensamiento y la Acción en la Vida de Juan Pablo Duarte*. Santo Domingo: Universidad Nacional Pedro Henríquez Ureña y Organización de Estados de Américas, 1979.

Pichardo, Bernardo. *Resumen de Historia Patria*. Barcelona: Altés, 1930. Reprint. 5th ed. Santo Domingo: Colección Pensamiento Dominicana, 1969.

Pierce, Edward L. *Memoirs and Letters of Charles Sumner*. 4 vols. Boston: Roberts Brothers, 1877–93.

Plummer, Brenda Gayle. *Haiti and the Great Powers, 1902–1915*. Baton Rouge and London: Louisiana State University Press, 1988.

Richardson, James D. *Messages and Papers of Presidents, 1789–1897*. 10 vols. Washington, D.C.: Government Printing Office, 1896–99.

Rodman, Selden. *Quisqueya*. Seattle: University of Washington Press, 1964.

Rodríguez Demorizi, Emilio. *Cesión de Santo Domingo a Francia*. Archivo General de la Nación. Santo Domingo: Impresona Dominicana, 1958.

———. *Documentos para la Historia de la República Dominicana*. 3 vols. Santo Domingo: Impresora Dominicana, 1959.

———. *Luperón y Hostos*. Santo Domingo: Editora Montalvo, 1939.

———. *Informe de la Comisión de Investigación de los E.U.A. en Santo Domingo en 1871*. Vol. 9, *Academia Dominicana de la Historia*. 10 vols. Santo Domingo: Montalvo, 1960.

———. *Papeles de General Santana*. Rome: Stab. Tipográfico, 1952.

————. *Relaciones Historicas de Santo Domingo.* 4 vols. Santo Domingo: Editora Montalvo, 1945.

————. *Santana y los Poetas de su Tiempo.* Santo Domingo: Editora del Caribe, 1969.

————. *Santo Domingo y la Gran Colombia: Bolívar y Núñez de Cáceres.* Vol. 33, *Academia Dominicana de la Historia.* Santo Domingo: Editora del Caribe, 1971.

Rodríguez Objío, Manuel. *Gregorio Luperón e Historia de la Restauración.* Santiago: Editorial el Diario, 1939.

Rood, Carlton Alexander. *A Dominican Chronicle.* 2d ed. Santo Domingo: Editora Corripio C. por A., 1986.

Schoenrich, Otto. *Santo Domingo, a Country with a Future.* New York: MacMillan Co., 1918.

Sevilla Soler, Rosario. *Santo Domingo: Tierra de la Frontera, 1750–1800.* Seville: Escuela de Estudios Hispano-Americanos, 1980.

Sherman, John. *Recollections of Forty Years in the House, Senate and Cabinet.* 2 vols. Chicago, New York: The Werner Company, 1895.

Suchlicki, Jaime. *Cuba from Columbus to Castro.* New York: Charles Scribners Sons, 1974.

Sumner, Charles. *Works of Charles Sumner.* 20 vols. Boston: Lee and Shepard, 1883.

Tansill, Charles Callan. *The United States and Santo Domingo, 1798–1873.* Baltimore: Johns Hopkins University Press, 1938.

————. *The Purchase of the Danish West Indies.* Baltimore: The Johns Hopkins University Press, 1932.

Thomas, Hugh. *Cuba: The Pursuit of Freedom.* New York: Harper and Row, 1971.

Trefousse, Hans G. *Carl Schurz.* Knoxville: University of Tennessee Press, 1982.

Vedovato, Cladio. *Politics, Foreign Trade and Economic Development: A Study of the Dominican Republic.* New York: St. Martin's Press, 1986.

Waddell, D. A. G. *The West Indies and the Guianas.* Englewood Cliffs, N.J.: Prentice-Hall, 1967.

Walker, Stanley. *Journey Toward the Sunlight.* New York: Caribbean Library, 1947.

Weinstein, Allen, and R. Jackson Wilson. *Freedom and Crisis.* 2 vols. New York: Random House, 1974.

Welles, Sumner. *Naboth's Vineyard: The Dominican Republic, 1844–1924.* 2 vols. New York: Payson and Clarke, 1928.

White, Andrew Dickson. *Autobiography.* 2 vols. New York: Century Co., 1905.

White, Horace. *Life of Lyman Trumbull.* New York: Houghton Mifflin Co., 1913.

Wiarda, Howard J., and Michael J. Kryzanek. *The Dominican Republic: A Caribbean Crucible.* Boulder, Colo.: Westview Press, 1982.

Wiktor, Christian L., ed. *Unperfected Treaties of the United States of America, 1776–1976.* 6 vols. Dobbs Ferry, N.Y.: Ocean Publications, 1976.

Williams, William Appleman. *Empire as a Way of Life.* New York: Oxford University Press, 1980.

Winch, Julie. *Philadelphia's Black Elite: Activism, Accommodation and the Struggle for Autonomy, 1787–1848.* Philadelphia: Temple University Press, 1988.

Wolf, John B. *France, 1815 to the Present.* New York: Prentice-Hall, 1940.

Woodward, W. E. *Meet General Grant.* New York: Horace Liveright, 1928.

Wriston, Henry M. *Executive Agents in American Foreign Relations.* Baltimore: Johns Hopkins University Press, 1929.

DOCTORAL DISSERTATIONS

Cross-Beras, Julio. "Clientelism, Dependency and Development in Nineteenth-century Dominican Republic." Ph.D. diss., Cornell University, 1980.

Themo, Elaine Marie. "The Process and Structures in the Development of Nationalism: A Case Study in the Dominican Republic." Ph.D. diss., American University, 1969.

Index